# Positive Parenting

# Positive Parenting

## How to Raise a Healthier and Happier Child (from birth to three years)

Alvin N. Eden, M.D.

Foreword by Lendon H. Smith, M.D.

With Photographs by Suzanne Szasz

THE BOBBS-MERRILL COMPANY, INC.   INDIANAPOLIS/NEW YORK

Published by The Bobbs-Merrill Company, Inc.
Indianapolis New York

Designed By: Jean Callan King
Manufactured in the United States of America

First Printing

**Library of Congress Cataloging in Publication Data**

Eden, Alvin N
  Positive parenting.

  1. Children — Management.  2. Child development.
3. Infants — Care and hygiene.  I. Title.
HQ769.E356     649'.1        80 – 680
ISBN 0 – 672 – 52662 – X

*To Elaine*
*and to our children, Robert and Elizabeth,*
*with love*

I want to thank Charles D. Cook, M.D., Professor and Chairman, Department of Pediatrics, State University of New York, Downstate Medical Center, for his helpful suggestions and comments.

Special thanks are due to my secretary, Catherine Hayes. This project could not have been completed without her untiring efforts and dedication.

# Author's Note

As I stated in my two previous books, *Growing Up Thin* and *Handbook for New Parents,* I firmly believe in the equality of the sexes. The English language still does not provide any graceful word to substitute for "his" and "her" or "he" and "she." Therefore, I have again decided to continue to alternate the pronouns used to describe gender, chapter by chapter, starting with the Introduction, thus giving equal time to both sexes. Please remember that these pronouns refer to your child, even if your baby is of the opposite sex—except, of course, where I make remarks that apply specifically to boys or girls. I start off the Introduction with "she," a decision made by the flip of a coin.

For similar reasons, "you" will refer to both mother and father, with one exception—the discussions relating to breast feeding.

# Table of Contents

# Foreword

I read and enjoyed Dr. Eden's *Positive Parenting* and found myself nodding in agreement on every page. He has an uncanny way of saying what I believe to be pediatric/parent truths. One can tell that he has examined a lot of babies and held a lot of parents' hands. His warmth and love for children are everywhere.

The chief attribute of this delightful, friendly, but medically sound tour through the difficult first few years is Dr. Eden's ability to calm parents (and grandparents) about those picayune irritations that should not be worrisome. He also alerts us with a rousing cry when a significant problem does appear (poisoning, abuse, neglect, severe infections).

He has a comforting, relaxing style; we are painlessly educated about the universal truths of child rearing. He lays out a plan for each age group — what to feed, what to say, how to stimulate, and what to worry about.

This book should be read twice. The first time through, you should read it for its ambiance. Then read the sections pertaining to the age of the child in question.

Child rearing should be fun. If all parents had *Positive Parenting* within reach, they would feel comfortable and confident. If parents do a good job with their children, those children might grow up to remember their parents' wedding anniversary.

*Lendon H. Smith, M.D.*

# Introduction

The great challenge of "positive parenting" is to raise a happy, healthy, emotionally stable child who will grow up to be successful in her work and in her interpersonal relationships. Every one of us wants the very best for our children, but how to achieve that goal is the big question. Although the right set of genes, good luck, and common sense all help, much more than that is needed to do the job. Helping parents nurture their child so that she may reach her full physical, emotional, and intellectual potential is my purpose in writing this book. That is indeed a tall order, and who am I to undertake it?

I have been a practicing pediatrician for the past twenty-five years and a father for the past twenty-four. Both of these roles have given me abundant experience with infants and children. I have had the opportunity of observing literally thousands of parents and children in action, and have been in the child-rearing profession long enough to come to some definite conclusions. There are right ways and wrong ways of raising children. Knowing what *not* to do is just as important as knowing what *to* do. All of us make many mistakes along the way, but the bottom line is to be able to realize when we are on the wrong track and to do something constructive about it. Mistakes in child-rearing are unavoidable, but repeating the same errors over and over again is not acceptable.

There is no question that the first three years of life are crucial to the emotional development of your youngster. More and more evidence has accumulated pointing to the fact that future physical and intellectual development also rests in large measure on what happens during these first few years. The experiences you give your child from birth to three years will greatly influence her intellectual, physical, and emotional development throughout her lifetime. If these experiences are not provided, the chances of achieving her full potential will be reduced. Let me give you an example of this. Two babies are born with equal genetic potential. Baby A is left in her crib most of the time to fend for herself, except for feeding, changing, and bathing. Baby B engages in stimulating play and activities, interacting during much of her waking time with her parents. Without question, Baby B will have a tremendous advantage over Baby A in terms of her school achievements and adult accomplishments. Baby B will also be more emotionally stable, happier, and more content.

This book, then, deals with the first three years of your child's life. A quick look at the chapter headings will give you an idea of how we have chosen to present our material. The first four chapters cover the first year of life in three-month increments: birth to three months, three to six months, six to nine months, and nine to twelve months. The next two chapters are devoted to the second year of life: twelve to eighteen months of age and eighteen to twenty-four months of age. The final chapter covers the two- to three-year-old period.

Each chapter will be quite specific in its recommendations and suggestions. Appropriate tables showing you growth and developmental milestones will be included in each chapter. It is my hope that this format will make it easier for you to achieve the goal of all parents; namely, to allow your child to achieve the very best possible that is in her, intellectually, emotionally, and physically.

My frame of reference in presenting this material is somewhat different from that of the child psychologist who deals almost exclusively with psychological and emotional development. As a pediatrician I must deal with the whole child, and this also includes her physical well-being. By physical well-being I do not mean only the prevention of disease. Rather, I espouse the concept of physical vigor and well-being based on proper exercise, nutrition, and the prevention of obesity. We will be dealing with these aspects of your child's physical development in each and every chapter. We will also discuss safety tips and accident prevention, chapter by chapter, in relation to your child's development, and we will try to explode many of the myths and old wives' tales associated with child rearing. For example, allowing a nine-month-old who enjoys standing and jumping up and down to do so, will *not* cause her to grow up bowlegged. On the contrary, it is good exercise and will help her develop agility and strength as she happily bounces around.

Before going any further, I should like to establish some ground rules. First of all, the concept of normal *ranges* of growth and development must be clearly understood. Just as in the case of reading a thermometer, when temperatures of 98.6° F. or 99.4° F. can be considered as falling within the normal *range,* there are normal *ranges* of developmental milestones. An infant who sits without support at seven months of age is just as normal as a six-month-old who does the same. You must always keep this concept in mind, both when reading the growth and development charts and when reading the text. It is a fact that many parents are overly concerned with how soon their babies start to talk. There are tremendous normal variations in language development from child to child. Some babies start to talk before their first birthday and others don't utter a word until they are two years old. The early talker is not necessarily the more intelligent child. The important thing to look for is how rapidly the child learns to *understand* words and phrases. Only when a child falls outside the normal *range* of growth and development should a parent become concerned and consult the doctor. Each child (including an identical twin) is unique and each one grows and develops at her own individual rate. This concept is so important that it will be repeated and emphasized over and over again as we go along.

This book was not written to make it easier for you to compare your child with your neighbor's child, nor, for that matter, to compare her with an older brother or sister. Comparing one to another is not only a waste of time, but may actually be destructive. Further, it has not been my intent in writing this book to make it easier for you to set unrealistic goals for your child. You may very well want your three-year-old to grow up to be a neurosurgeon or another O. J. Simpson, but my best advice is to keep those expectations to yourself. Nor is my purpose to motivate you to spend every waking moment figuring out ways to push and pressure your child along into becoming the "best" in everything. Overburdening your baby will actually slow down her development.

I have not written this book to substitute for or infringe upon your baby's doctor. It is extremely important that you find the proper physician for your child, either a pediatrician or a family physician who takes care of infants and children. Aside from the doctor's experience, credentials, and hospital appointments, he or she must be available when needed. No matter how good his or her training, if the doctor you have selected or his or her substitute is never around, this is unacceptable. Emergencies do arise and they must be met. If you find that you never can communicate with the doctor, especially during times of emergency, you would be wise to think about making a change.

The so-called "well-baby" visits scheduled every four to six weeks during your baby's first year, and less frequently after that, are misnamed. Too many parents believe that the only reason for these periodic checkups is to allow the doctor to administer the various "shots" (immunizations) needed. While it is true that immunizations are essential for optimal health, this is not the main reason for these examinations. Only through these regular office visits can your baby's doctor assess your child's growth and development and pick up any slight deviation from the normal early enough that effective treatment can be given. These examinations also allow the doctor to diagnose an illness that you may not be able to recognize. Your doctor will also check your baby's vision and hearing. Among the major causes of poor academic achievement are impaired vision and impaired hearing. If a defect is picked up early enough, it can be corrected more easily. And, important for your own feelings of confidence and security, during these sessions you will have the opportunity to ask your doctor questions and discuss any problems that may have arisen since the last visit.

Many well-meaning parents practice "crisis medicine." This means that the only time the infant or child is taken to the physician is when she is ill. This is absolutely wrong and can lead to irreparable and irreversible damage. By keeping up the so-called "well-baby" and "well-child" visits to your doctor, you will give your child a much better opportunity to develop optimally in all areas.

Finally, I have not written this book to help instill guilt. There is no question that many parents are anxious and unsure of themselves. It is my hope that reading the information in my book will allay much of this fear and insecurity. All that parents can be expected to give is the very best they have in them and no more. It would be unrealistic and foolish of me to expect anybody to follow to the very last detail each and every suggestion and guideline presented. Let me assure you that there are many successful methods of raising children. I am simply offering my approach for your consideration. I believe that following many of my recommendations will make it easier for you to be a "quality" or positive parent. If you find that some of what I say is impossible for you to follow, or if you disagree with certain of my suggestions, or if your baby's doctor has different ideas, so be it.

All authorities in child development pretty much agree that parents do not have to be well-educated or enormously intelligent in order to give their child the best possible start in life. There is really no reason to feel inadequate or upset if you do not have a Ph.D. from Harvard. As a matter of fact, some of the best and most successful parents I have ever known have had a minimum of formal education.

It is not easy to be a parent today. The American family as we know it is under tremendous economic and social pressure. By the mid-1970s more than one-half of mothers with school-age children and more than one-third of mothers with preschool-age children were working outside the home. The figures are even higher now at the start of the 1980s. Further, over one in three marriages result in divorce. It has been estimated that four out of every ten children who were born in 1970 will spend part of their childhood in a single-parent family.

Many among us believe that the concept of "family" has become outdated and obsolete. This group argues that the only real and important entity is the individual. I don't agree. As far as I am concerned, the family still remains the most important unit in our society. The interrelationships, or "family life," that tie the various members of a family together are the vital core of our society. I believe that these family interrelationships between parents and children are critical to the optimum development of the child. Various outside pressures put an enormous strain on the family. Both mothers and fathers are forced to spend many hours away from their homes and their children. It is therefore even more important that the time spent with the child be "quality" time.

Not enough attention or credit is given to parents who provide much of what a child needs in order to grow up to be happy and productive. I agree completely with Dr. Spock, who decries the ignominious standing given to the status of child rearing in the United States today. In recent years much has been written about all the mothers and fathers who are neither competent nor qualified. Many of these so-called authorities preach the concept of having "experts" assume the child-rearing role instead of the parents. The unhappy result of all this is that more and more parents feel frustrated and helpless, believing that they lack the intelligence and skills to raise their own children. For this reason more and more men and women are making the decision not to have any children.

This gradual erosion of our family structure is raising havoc with our children, and the trend must be reversed. I cannot emphasize strongly enough that there is nothing more important than the "family." Bringing up your own child and taking pride and satisfaction in doing the best job possible is what it's all about. The obligation to be a real parent to your child should be, but unfortunately often is not, the most powerful drive in today's society. The prime responsibility of parents is to work together in order to raise their children properly and to help build strong family ties. Character is built; nobody is born jealous or selfish. Parents should learn to use the word "our" rather than "my." Although it should be obvious, many parents do not realize that their children learn by example. Even small infants are attuned and responsive to what goes on around them. I will never forget talking to the parents of a two-year-old boy whose entire vocabulary at the time consisted of "shud up" and "shid." By the time he was three he could pronounce his t's.

During the first few years it is particularly important that a close, nonrejecting, stimulating, trusting, and responsive relationship be established between parents and child. If this close and enduring relationship is not developed, lasting detrimental effects on the future emotional and intellectual growth of the child may result. Many studies have clearly shown that early exposure to factors that stimulate a child's interests and motivate her to higher and higher achievement influence and affect her level of functioning when she starts school. Parents should do everything possible to provide their children with both an environment conducive to exploration and the time for these children to share their ideas and accomplishments with them. This kind of environment is a most important ingredient in the development of intelligence. A baby's intellectual development is closely tied up with her feelings. The two really cannot be separated. Therefore, in order to develop to the fullest intellectually, the child not only needs activities and stimulation, but also the confidence to know that she can do it (self-esteem). She must also believe that these activities are worth doing. This requires you to show not only love, but also pride in her accomplishments while at the same time not expecting too much too soon. You can never encourage your child too often or too much and you never should stop showing her and telling her how proud you are of her achievements. Building up sufficient self-esteem and self-worth early on in your child's life is probably the most important way to nurture and guarantee her future emotional health and well-being. If this is successfully instilled, your child will be well on her way to a happy, fulfilling life. A truly loving parent should share her child's discoveries and enjoyments. Be very careful not to put down your child, but rather praise her for her accomplishments. Remind your child at every opportunity how much you love her, how proud you are of her, and how happy you are to have her.

The right attitude and good intentions give you a good start. But it takes more than that to be a truly positive parent. It takes a detailed understanding of your child's growth and development. It requires separating fact from fiction. It requires specific knowledge, whether it be about nutrition, safety, toys, games, activities, bonding, trust, or self-esteem — step by step, age by age. Learning what to expect and when to expect it and what you can do to help as your child rapidly grows from infancy to three years of age, ready and equipped to face school and the outside world, is what you will gain from this book.

You are competent for the task. There is nothing complicated, magical, or mystical about child rearing. Parents need specific guidelines and direction, depending on the particular age of the child. This book is my attempt to help you reach your goal of giving your child the very best possible start in order to achieve her maximum physical, intellectual, and emotional growth and potential. You will never have a more satisfying and important challenge.

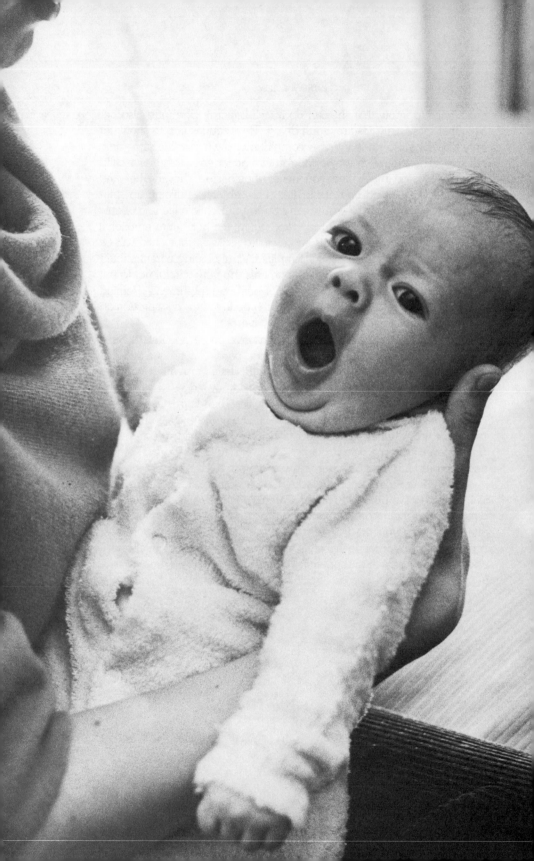

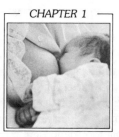

# CHAPTER 1

# Birth to Three Months

The big day has finally arrived. After nine months of waiting, your baby is born. This is a hectic period for all concerned. The proper equipment and supplies must be on hand in order to satisfy the physical needs of the new baby. Drastic changes in sleep schedules and work loads for both mother and father are the order of the day. Sleeping late on a Sunday morning and reading leisurely through the newspaper are things of the past. It isn't easy to allocate time properly so that everything gets done. This is all obvious, and there really is no reason to dwell on this aspect in any great detail. What it all comes down to is the establishment of proper priorities.

If you are a fastidious, compulsive homemaker, you will simply have to let your housework go if this interferes with your spending enough time relating to and interacting with the new baby. It is easier and more satisfactory for all if both the mother and father share the various new chores right from the start. If this happens, the "family" will be starting off in the right direction. There is nothing unmanly about a father changing his baby's diaper or giving him a bath. I have been pleased to observe that in recent years more and more new young fathers are participating more fully in actively caring for their new infants. Nonetheless, there are still too many new mothers who are overly possessive of their newborns and always talk about "my" baby. This type of mother makes it more difficult for the father to share in the raising of their new baby, even if he really is anxious to do so. I would like to remind you that all of us are born with forty-six chromosomes, twenty-three of which come from the mother and an equal number from the father. All things being equal, a new baby is entitled to the loving care of both mother and father. Such a baby has a distinct advantage over the baby who has only his mother to care for his needs.

I have been upset through the years by the fact that many new parents do not realize just how important these first three months are for their baby's future emotional and intellectual development. The emphasis of child rearing during this period is usually placed almost exclusively on the physical needs of the infant—feeding, changing, cleaning, bathing, and the like. Of course, these areas are important but the new infant has many other needs that are just as important. Many parents are completely unaware of the fact that the first three months of an infant's life comprise a period of not only rapid physical but rapid intellectual and emotional growth as well.

Strong evidence indicates that infants from very early in life have many adaptive capabilities. A baby is not a lump of clay to be molded and shaped by his parents; each baby has a complex personality and each is unique in his potential. A baby starts developing from the first moment he is born. An infant's developmental powers come from within. These powers obviously are helped by the environment surrounding him. Not only is the infant influenced by the environment around him, but he in turn influences the environment as well. The earlier parents realize this, the better. During the first three months of life, infants frequently smile before they are smiled at, look at people before they are looked at, and, of course, communicate by crying. The result is that an infant attracts the attention of the people around him. By their own efforts infants often increase the degree of stimulation of their environment. This is a difficult concept for many parents to accept, but if you do, it will help you tremendously in your child-rearing activities. As the mother of a two-month-old girl recently told me, "You know, Dr. Eden, Amanda is a real person and very nice. She's fun to have around." I wish more new parents would feel this way.

The simplest way to look at it is that during this period almost all of your baby's needs can be taken care of right in your arms. His main physical need is proper nutrition, and a baby should be held while being fed. His emotional needs can also mainly be satisfied by holding, and a good part of his intellectual stimulation is achieved by playing with him as you hold him in your arms. New babies respond to warmth and cuddling. Security and comfort are conveyed through the feel of the mother's or father's body. Love is also conveyed through touch, so don't skimp with the holding and hugging. Love is also conveyed by verbal contact—tone of voice, a point many parents do not realize. A newborn hears clearly right from the start.

A normal infant makes rapid and dramatic progress in growth and development physically, emotionally, and intellectually during the first three months. In the growth and development charts that follow, I have listed some of the important developmental milestones that your baby will achieve. As I have already stated, there are normal *ranges,* and each and every baby progresses at a different rate. These charts are simply guidelines so that any large deviation should be called to the attention of your baby's doctor. One point to remember is that these charts (and the charts in subsequent chapters) refer to full-term infants. A premature baby often will grow and develop at a slower rate and may take up to two years or longer to catch up with the full-term infant.

The growth and development charts are divided into three sections:
1. Physical or motor
2. Emotional or social
3. Mental or intellectual

There is often an overlap between social and mental milestones and they really cannot be separated in any meaningful way. Therefore, the same activity may be listed twice. Since advances are so rapid during the first year of life, the charts of this chapter and the following three chapters are broken down into one-month increments. These charts are incomplete in the sense that they do not attempt to list everything your baby will be doing each month. However, they do list what I consider many of the most important milestones. Becoming familiar with what to expect and when to expect it will make the specific suggestions and recommendations that follow more meaningful and easier to carry out.

3

## Birth – 3 Months

## GROWTH AND DEVELOPMENT
*Physical (Motor)*

### Birth — 1 Month

1. Thrusts out arms and legs.
2. In sitting position, head falls backward or forward.
3. On stomach, can lift head slightly and briefly.
4. Usually holds hands in fistlike position.
5. Rolls slightly to side while on back.

### 1 — 2 Months

1. On stomach, lifts and holds head up off surface.
2. Brings hands together in front.
3. On back, turns head to side.
4. Makes voluntary movements of arms and legs.
5. When held in sitting position, holds head fairly steady.
6. Begins voluntary grasping.
7. May hold object for a few seconds.
8. May start to swipe at nearby objects.

### 2 — 3 Months

1. On stomach, can lift both head and chest up off surface.
2. Usually holds hands open.
3. Able to sit supported with head held fairly steady.
4. Actively moves arms and legs, usually both arms and both legs together.
5. Starts to reach for nearby objects, usually without success.
6. May grasp a rattle placed in fingers.
7. Turns head efficiently from one side to another.
8. When held steady, starts to support part of weight on legs and stands.

*Note:* These charts are based on average *ranges* of growth and development; many normal babies perform and achieve either sooner or later than indicated.

## Birth – 3 Months

## GROWTH AND DEVELOPMENT
### *Emotional (Social)*

### Birth – 1 Month

1. Pays attention to sounds, especially familiar voices.
2. Stares at faces and objects with vacant expression.
3. Starts eye-to-eye contact.
4. Usually stops crying when held and cuddled.
5. Cries for help and when in pain.

### 1 – 2 Months

1. Smiles when you smile or play with him.
2. Smiles on his own; start of showing happiness.
3. Squeals and makes throaty and cooing sounds.
4. Enjoys bath and being held, handled, and played with.
5. Listens attentively to various sounds.
6. Quiets down when held or in response to familiar voice or face.
7. Can quiet self with sucking breast, bottle, or pacifier.

### 2 – 3 Months

1. Smiles easily and spontaneously.
2. Laughs, squeals, chuckles, gurgles, and coos.
3. Alertly turns head toward speaking or singing voices or other sounds.
4. Recognizes mother or other primary care person.
5. Starts to try to attract the attention of anybody around.
6. Need for social stimulation more and more apparent; e.g., when talked to, responds with various sounds.
7. Begins to be able to distinguish different speech sounds from other sounds.
8. Feels upset and protests when left alone.

*Note:* These charts are based on average *ranges* of growth and development; many normal babies perform and achieve either sooner or later than indicated.

5

## Birth – 3 Months

GROWTH AND DEVELOPMENT
*Mental (Intellectual)*

### Birth — 1 Month

1. Can focus eyes poorly.
2. Vague, vacant expression on face while awake.
3. Quiets when being held.
4. Can fix gaze on light or large nearby object.
5. Cries for help.

### 1 — 2 Months

1. Can focus eyes more efficiently.
2. Stares at surroundings, preferring person to object.
3. Can follow light or moving object to midline.
4. Becomes animated and excited when anticipating activity, such as feeding.
5. Associates a particular person with a particular activity; e.g., mother and feeding.
6. Studies own hand movements.

### 2 — 3 Months

1. Begins to demonstrate memory.
2. Starts to recognize and differentiate various family members.
3. Follows with his eyes from one side all the way around to the other side of his head.
4. Can look at one object or person and then to another.
5. Explores his own mouth, face, and other parts of his body with his hands.
6. Can turn head and neck efficiently to look for source of sound.
7. Becomes bored and irritated when not sufficiently stimulated with activities.

Note: These charts are based on average *ranges* of growth and development; many normal babies perform and achieve either sooner or later than indicated.

With the growth and development charts in mind, I'd like to go on to the specific recommendations that will get your infant off to the best possible start physically, emotionally, and mentally.

## PHYSICAL (MOTOR) DEVELOPMENT

## NUTRITION

Proper nutrition is most important in helping your baby to reach optimal physical health and well-being during these first three months. Unfortunately, many of our current infant feeding practices are faulty, often leading to obesity, iron-deficiency anemia, and increased strain on the kidneys. The possible long-term implications of inadequate and faulty nutrition may include coronary heart disease, high blood pressure, and adult obesity.

The ideal way to feed an infant during the first three months and beyond is to breast feed. Human milk has been shown to be ideally suited to the infant's nutritional needs during the entire first year of life. Furthermore, there is strong evidence that in addition to being nutritionally perfect, breast milk contains antibodies that protect your baby against certain viral and bacterial infections, especially those involving the gastrointestinal tract. Some preliminary results of large-scale investigations support the theory that breast-fed babies may be better able to handle cholesterol in later life than those who were bottle fed. Breast feeding is also easy, economical, and hygienic.

The 1970s witnessed a new interest in breast feeding. Compared to twenty years ago, twice as many new mothers decided to breast feed their infants. However, there is still a large dropout rate, so that by three months of age about one-half of the breast-feeding mothers have stopped. This results primarily from social factors. More and more mothers work outside the home, which makes extended breast feeding difficult to accomplish. Part of the solution rests with the establishment by industry of breast-feeding stations in offices, factories, and the like, and it is to be hoped this will become a reality in the future. But as of today, such facilities are scarce. So what is the breast-feeding working mother to do?

If at all possible, I would strongly recommend that you breast feed your baby for at least the first three months of life. There are very few valid medical reasons for not breast feeding. It is the best way to satisfy all the nutritional needs of a baby. Many mothers make the mistake of not thinking enough during their pregnancy about whether or not they want to breast feed. This is the sensible time to decide. But usually the decision is made only after the baby is born. As a pediatrician, there are times when I do not see an infant until he is brought into my office at

7

one month of age. Obviously, it is too late then to discuss the advantages of breast feeding with the parents if the baby is already on the bottle. When I do have the opportunity of examining the newborn in the hospital, I do my best to encourage the new mother to breast feed her baby. What I am about to write will not sit well with some of my obstetrical colleagues, but I believe that as a group, obstetricians are not as knowledgeable and interested as they should be in presenting the case for breast feeding during the pregnancy. Of course, the ultimate decision must rest with the mother, but how can she make a sensible choice of breast versus bottle if she is not made aware of the many advantages of breast feeding?

**Myth:** *Breast feeding will damage the contour of the breasts and will cause them to sag.* There is absolutely no evidence that this happens. If a mother maintains her proper weight and does the appropriate exercises, breast feeding will not change the shape of her breasts in any way.

When breast feeding is unsuccessful, inappropriate because of life style, stopped before three months of age, or simply if the choice is made to bottle feed, there is no reason to feel guilty about it. Although I always encourage mothers to breast feed, I disagree with those in the probreast-feeding community who take the position that it is a crime not to do so. This overzealous, highly militant group has not yet come right out and advocated prison for such a mother, but it sometimes comes close. The commercially available formulas we have today provide the most rational and desirable alternative to breast milk for meeting all the infant's nutritional needs. Although they are not identical to it, they are quite similar to breast milk in their nutrient mix. In addition to being very close to breast milk in the amounts of carbohydrate, fat, and protein they contain, commercial formulas also have comparable concentrations of minerals and vitamins. There is no question that from the nutritional point of view, babies do beautifully on these formulas.

For the bottle-fed infant, the Committee on Nutrition of the American Academy of Pediatrics recommends that an iron-fortified formula be used from the start and that it be continued for at least the first six months of life. Their rationale for this is to prevent iron-deficiency anemia. In my own practice, I see many bottle-feeding mothers use commercially available formulas without iron, and I believe that this is perfectly acceptable if iron is added to the diet at the appropriate time. The whole subject of iron-deficiency anemia will be discussed more fully in the next two chapters, since this form of anemia is not a problem during the first three months of a baby's life.

9

Whether you breast feed or bottle feed, the important point to remember is *not to overfeed* your baby.

**Myth:** *A fat baby is a healthy baby.* Many mothers and fathers still hold to this mistaken belief, but it simply is not true. Please do not fall into this trap. My first book, *Growing Up Thin,* dealt with my approach to the prevention of obesity in infants and children. I feel very strongly about the importance of not ever allowing your baby to get fat. The evidence is quite clear that obesity, whether in an infant, child, or adult, is unhealthy. Fat babies accumulate excess numbers of fat cells which stay with them the rest of their lives. My experience as well as the experience of others in the field shows that fat babies more often grow up to become fat adults than do thin or normal-weight babies. I will be returning to this subject in subsequent chapters. Overfeeding an infant supplies unnecessary extra calories which inevitably lead to deposits of fat that hinder optimum physical development. If you avoid overfeeding from the very beginning, you have a better chance of sparing your child all the unpleasantness and the health hazards of growing up fat.

How can an infant be overfed? One way is by not allowing your baby to decide when the feeding is over. I find this occurring more often among bottle-feeding mothers than among the breast-feeding group. The reason is that the bottle-feeding mother knows exactly how many ounces of formula she started with, and come hell or high water she will see to it that every last drop gets down the baby's throat. The breast-feeding mother has no way of knowing exactly how many ounces her infant took in, and so the feeding stops when the baby is satisfied and satiated.

An important point to keep in mind is that it takes at least three hours for an infant's stomach to empty after an adequate feeding. Therefore, if your baby is crying one or two hours after a feeding, it is unlikely that he is crying because he is hungry. Many new parents automatically assume that every time a baby cries he is hungry. This just is not so. Infants cry for many other reasons. They cry when they are lonely, thirsty for water, gassy, or cranky, and sometimes they cry with no apparent explanation. The fact that an infant will take some of the bottle or suck on the breast does not necessarily mean that he was really hungry. Sucking is a normal reflex in all infants. Overfeeding is an inappropriate feeding practice. In the long run it can lead to obesity, and along with obesity comes inactivity. This all leads to much less than optimal physical health.

It is relatively easy for you to recognize if and when your infant is being overfed. During the first three months of life a baby should gain about one and a half pounds per month. If he is gaining well over two pounds each month, there is little question that he is being overfed. An infant who is bottle fed and who is gaining weight too rapidly can be slowed down by giving him formula diluted with water. For example, if your baby is taking six ounces per feeding, each bottle can be made up with four ounces of formula and two ounces of water. Before diluting the formula you should, of course, consult with your baby's physician. If he agrees that your baby is gaining weight too fast he may advise you to cut down on caloric intake. It is more difficult to do something about excessive weight gain in an infant who is being breast fed. We still have not figured out a way to dilute breast milk. However, some studies show that many of the breast-fed babies who have gained excessive amounts of weight during the first few months of life slim down more rapidly later on than bottle-fed babies with the same degree of obesity. We do not know why this happens. Suffice it to say that there is less to worry about with an overweight breast-fed baby than with an overweight bottle-fed baby.

It has been my experience that the incidence of obesity among bottle-fed babies is greater than among the breast-feeding group. I believe that this can be explained by the fact that the average breast-feeding mother is less frantic and tense and tends to overfeed less often. Further, breast-feeding mothers usually begin giving their infants solid foods later than bottle-feeding mothers.

An infant should be kept on a diet consisting exclusively of breast milk or commercially available formula for at least the first three months of life. It is not uncommon for mothers to switch their babies to cow's milk sometime during this period. This is absolutely wrong and should never be done. As a matter of fact, infants should not be given cow's milk for at least the first six months of life, and preferably should remain on breast milk or formula for the entire first year. There are good and valid reasons for this recommendation, and I will discuss them in detail in subsequent chapters. Besides breast milk or formula, in the first three months an infant requires one of the multivitamin drop preparations, and perhaps fluoride and some water between feedings. I would consider this the ideal way to feed your infant. Such an approach will go a long way in keeping him strong and healthy without putting on extra pounds to slow him down.

A dramatic decrease in the incidence of dental caries and a reduction of family dental expenses are both well-established results of fluoride administration in childhood. The Committee on Nutrition of the American Academy of Pediatrics recently published new recommendations regarding fluoride supplementation for infants and children. They recommend fluoride supplementation in very early infancy, starting at two weeks and continuing until sixteen years of age, with the amount of supplemental fluoride dependent on the fluoride content of the drinking water in the community. I would suggest that you check the status of the water supply in your community with regard to its fluoride concentration by calling your Department of Health. If you find that your water supply does not contain sufficient fluoride, your infant will require extra fluoride by mouth. This can be given in the form of fluoride drops or in combination with a multivitamin preparation. The daily dose of fluoride will be determined by the level of fluoride in the water supply; this holds true both for breast-fed and formula-fed babies. My advice would be to check with your baby's physician, who should be able to tell you if extra fluoride is necessary, and if it is, the proper dose for your infant.

**Myth:** *Solid food helps a baby sleep through the night.* Despite what you may have heard to the contrary, there is no real evidence that this is true. Just about all the authorities on infant nutrition agree that for at least the first three months, solid food is not only unnecessary for desired growth and development, but actually is contraindicated. The too-early introduction of cereals, fruits, and the like supplies the infant with unnecessary extra calories and also may cause colic and other gastrointestinal problems. There is even some evidence that this too-early introduction of solids predisposes a child to food allergies and perhaps even respiratory allergies later on in life. In my own practice, I start the infants under my care on solid foods at around four months of age, and in the next chapter I will give you my specific suggestions and schedules. It is difficult to convince many parents and it is especially difficult to convince grandparents that solid foods should be withheld during the first three months. Nevertheless, your infant will be better off if you go along with this recommendation. This reminds me of an interesting telephone conversation I recently had with a new mother who called me up at five o'clock one morning asking me if she could start her eight-day-old baby girl on some cereal. I confess that I was not quite as pleasant as I could have been in answering her. What I said (for which I apologized later on) was the following: "No, you certainly can't start the baby on cereal. However, I certainly would recommend pizza with sausages and anchovies."

Before going on to exercises for your infant up to the age of three months, let me take care of two other common misconceptions:

**Myth:** *Air conditioning is harmful for my baby.* Wrong. Your baby's temperature is no different from your own. If the temperature in your house is such that you are more comfortable in an air-conditioned room, the same holds true for your infant. Nowadays most hospital nurseries are air-conditioned, so there is no reason for you to believe that air-conditioning is harmful in any way. Your baby will be much more comfortable and content in a cool (not cold) environment rather than in a hot, stuffy room. A temperature setting between 65° F. and 70° F. is ideal.

**Myth:** *Flash bulbs should not be used to take pictures of new babies.* Wrong again. There is no reason not to use flash bulbs since they do not damage your infant's eyes. Go right ahead and snap away. I hope your photographs turn out sharp and clear!

### EXERCISE

Aside from proper feeding practices, you can do a good deal more to help your new baby develop strength, agility, and muscle tone. Remember that your new baby is not a fragile object to be handled with care because it may break. On the contrary, new babies are quite sturdy and well engineered. There is no reason to be afraid of handling or moving them around. Your main precaution should be to support your infant's head for the first month or so, when it is quite wobbly. Infants are most often carried around in the so-called burping position up on your shoulder. I would suggest that you carry him around in different positions as well. This helps strengthen his large muscles. An infant seat or a pack-sack can be used for this purpose. The baby can sometimes be positioned face forward and sometimes face backward. Not only will this help his physical development, but it is more interesting for the infant as well. Strengthening the infant's neck muscles and helping him to achieve good head control should also be part of his activity schedule. The way to do this is to place him on his stomach a number of times each day. This will give him the opportunity to learn to lift his head off the surface. There is no question that babies love to be handled, bounced up and down, and exercised. The earlier you start, the stronger and more agile your baby will become. There is an additional exercise that is useful. When the infant is lying on his back, his legs can be exercised by pumping them gently as if he is riding a bicycle. You will

13

find that along with his enjoyment of the activity, all the muscles in his lower extremities will be strengthened.

Various crib devices are useful in stimulating physical activity. They need not be elaborate, and you can make them yourself. If you do, be certain that they are sturdy and solid. There are a number of different crib devices that can be purchased. One example is a cradle gym. These devices, with rings and bells attached, are hung over the crib. A baby will start to swipe and reach at around two to three months of age, and this gives him an excellent opportunity to exercise. Incidentally, he also will be very pleased with the noises he produces when he actually hits his crib device.

Optimal physical development requires more than just feeding, bathing, and changing the infant. It requires proper feeding practices as well as exercising and handling and moving the baby around. A flabby, inactive infant is not as healthy as a toned-up, active one. A fat baby is not as healthy as a thin or normal-weight baby. The future physical well-being of your infant begins right now.

Safety is a major factor in caring for young children. Thus, in this chapter and in all subsequent chapters I will list a number of important safety tips immediately after the section dealing with the physical aspects of your child's development. I am sure you would agree that a serious accident such as a severe burn or the ingestion of a poison will adversely affect and tragically, sometimes permanently, interfere with optimal physical health and well-being.

## SAFETY TIPS

***Never smoke when carrying your baby.*** You may wonder why I have included this tip, as it seems so obvious. Please believe me when I tell you that through the years I have had to treat many small infants who have been severely burned by a lighted cigarette. While we are on the subject of smoking, I would like to make a general plea to all parents to stop smoking. This would not only be best for the health of your small baby, but also for your own welfare. A number of studies, both in the United States and in Scandinavia, have proved conclusively that during the first year of a child's life he is particularly vulnerable to respiratory infections. It has been shown that the infant living in a house with smokers has a much greater chance of being hospitalized before his first birthday because of a severe respiratory infection than the baby who lives in a smoke-free environment. Perhaps this knowledge will motivate you enough to give up cigarettes. I would also advise you to cut out cigarettes during pregnancy, since it has been shown that smoking can damage the developing fetus.

*Never leave your baby unattended while he is on any surface from which he can fall.* Recently I had to hospitalize a two-and-a-half-month-old who suddenly decided to turn over for the very first time. Unfortunately, this happened while he was on a dressing table when his mother went to answer the telephone. The result was that he fell off the table, landed on his head, and suffered a cerebral concussion. Happily, he recovered without any permanent damage.

*Never allow your infant to ride in an automobile while being held in your arms.* This method of automobile traveling has been proved unsafe. An infant seat specifically designed for automobile travel should always be used, and it should be one in which the baby faces backwards. Two of the popular and safe models are the Infant Carrier and the Infant Love Seat. The trip home from the hospital nursery should be the first time your infant uses an appropriate automobile infant seat. Unfortunately, I do not see this happening often enough and the result has been many accidents involving infants that could have been prevented.

*Hearing.* Although not specifically a safety tip, I want to include danger signals related to hearing difficulties during the first three months of an infant's life, because poor hearing can threaten a child's well-being in many ways.
  1. Your newborn baby does not startle in response to a sharp clap within three to six feet of him.
  2. Your two-month-old does not awaken from a sudden loud noise in his room.
If either is the case with your baby, notify your doctor about it immediately.

## EMOTIONAL (SOCIAL) DEVELOPMENT

The two key words at the core of starting your new baby on the road to optimum emotional development are *bonding* and *trust*. The development of bonding and trust describe what your most important job will be during the first three months of your infant's life.

15

## BONDING

What do we mean by *bonding?* This is a relatively new concept in parenting but is of prime importance. In recent years a good deal of convincing evidence has accumulated emphasizing the significance of the infant's early emotional and social attachment to and interaction with his mother and father. This bonding process appears to be crucial in determining many future aspects of the child's personality and the relationships he will establish throughout his life with his parents and with other people. It has been shown in some excellently designed investigations that as little as sixteen hours of close contact between the mother and infant during the first three days of life can modify the emotional quality of the relationship between them in ways that can be determined and detected as long as one year later.

From the very first time you hold your new baby, you are starting to communicate your feelings, and your newborn gets the message. The emotional bonds that are created between newborn and parent seem to be similar to the process of "imprinting" in animals, the process by which the young of many vertebrate species identify the social milieu to which they belong and to which they will turn for interaction. We know much more about animal "imprinting" than we know about newborn bonding in humans. The critical periods for "imprinting" have been established in certain animal species. We are uncertain as to what critical periods exist in man, but it is clear that the first few days and weeks are extremely important. Largely as a result of our new knowledge about the importance of bonding, increased attention is now being paid to the circumstances surrounding delivery and newborn care in the hospital. Having fathers present during the delivery is gradually becoming more accepted. Some hospitals now allow fathers to be present during caesarean sections. Rooming-in arrangements for mothers and their babies are being made in more and more obstetrical hospital units.

Contact between mother and infant immediately after birth is not necessarily essential to the development of positive effective attachments later on. Infants who miss this earliest bonding experience are not necessarily doomed to a life consisting of poor relationships. There is no reason to be upset if, for whatever reason, you weren't close to your newborn right after delivery. As long as you are aware of the need, you can take steps to compensate later, if you cannot be close to your child immediately after birth.

The most reasonable way to look at bonding is that although it can't begin too early, whenever it starts it is a continuing and ongoing process which never stops. There is strong evidence that the entire first three months of life are crucial in terms of bonding. The lack of sensory stimulation — holding, touching, talking to, singing to, laughing with the baby — is called maternal or paternal deprivation. Without such stimulation and interaction, the deprived infant will find it difficult and sometimes impossible to form positive emotional attachments to other people later on in life. Most authorities agree that social and emotional deprivation cannot be separated from intellectual deprivation. It has also been found that a mother who does not develop a close and intense attachment to her infant by the end of the third month has already clearly indicated to the child that he is unwanted. This can have devastating effects in the future.

Before leaving this discussion of bonding, I'd like to reemphasize the fact that there is now strong evidence that fathers can bond just as effectively and meaningfully as mothers with their newborn infants. Paternal bonding has not been given the attention it deserves until very recently. There is nothing magical or unique about mother-infant bonding, though a large segment of the population believes there is. Unfortunately, the role of the father in terms of newborn care has been played down through the years. The stereotype of the father whose main and primary function during the first couple of years is to be the breadwinner of the family, and who leaves the day-to-day child rearing exclusively to his wife, is no longer acceptable. As a matter of fact, effective fatherhood really should begin during the prenatal period, before the baby is born. The degree of a man's concern and involvement with the physical and emotional health of his pregnant spouse and the unborn baby often will be a good predictor of just how effective he will be as a father after the baby is born. Double bonding, involving both mother and father, is the best way to start the infant on the road to future emotional stability and intellectual accomplishment.

## TRUST

As far as the infant's emotional needs during the first three months of life are concerned, the other important key word is *trust*. It is clear that a feeling of trust should be instilled in your infant starting on day one. It is very important that your baby gets the feeling that the world around him is reliable and that all his needs will be met. A newborn really only has one way to communicate his needs to you, and that is by crying. Rather than worrying about your baby's crying, you should consider crying a very useful tool. I would disagree with those who take the position that it is all right to allow an infant to cry without responding in order not to "spoil" him. This attitude certainly will do very little in building up trust between you and your newborn. Babies cry for many reasons: hunger, thirst, gassiness, being wet or soiled, loneliness, over-tiredness. Babies have different cries to express different needs, and this is their first step in learning to communicate. Your main job is to become attuned to your baby and to his needs. In most cases this is not too difficult. It usually takes only a few days or weeks for you to be able to recognize why he is crying so that you can respond appropriately. There will be times when you will not be able to recognize and understand why your infant is crying, and it becomes a matter of trial and error for you to solve the problem. Let me assure you that almost every infant is unhappy and irritable some of the time. This is inevitable and so you need not assume any guilt. When you don't know why your baby is crying or is fussy and irritable, my best advice is to pick him up and hold him. This approach will not spoil him. Rather, it will start to build up his trust in you, and nothing is more important than that.

Let's get down to specifics.

**Respond to your infant's needs.** If he is crying, hold him. Newborn infants are relatively helpless and can only communicate their needs to you by crying. No, you won't "spoil" your baby by picking him up when he is crying during these first three months.

**Spend time with him.** New babies are social, responsive, and need your company. The time you spend with your infant is vital to his emotional and psychological development, and you should be happy to want to share this time with him.

**Communicate with him.** Although the new infant does not understand the meaning of your words, he does understand and respond to your tone of voice. Try very hard to speak to him in a soothing, gentle manner, and smile and laugh with him and sing to him.

**Hold him — the more the better.** The best way you can convey your feeling of love to your infant is through touch.

**Feeding.** Breast feeding is the ideal way to satisfy your baby's emotional needs. The close contact that occurs during breast feeding does much to establish trust between you, and is a continuing and ongoing bonding process. Bottle feeding can also be a time for building up trust and for bonding. It is most important to *hold* your baby when you feed him a bottle of formula. There is no excuse for *ever* propping up a bottle. Every baby needs the security and love that go along with a feeding which includes holding and touching.

**Build up your baby's self-esteem.** It is never too early for this. Each and every achievement and accomplishment for your infant should be properly acknowledged. For example, if your baby learns to hit his cradle gym, he will respond with joy to the noise and motion. At such times you should also respond with joy to his achievement and tell him so with a hug and a kiss and a smile. Your reaction will reinforce his pride in having learned the skill and will go a long way toward making your baby think well of himself. You may be surprised that I am using terms such as "pride" and "accomplishment" and "self-esteem" in describing what a two- or three-month-old can feel. Don't be. The sooner you realize that your infant's emotional needs are no different from a five-year-old's and no different from your own, for that matter, the better for both of you.

## MENTAL (INTELLECTUAL) DEVELOPMENT

It would be safe to say that most parents believe that not much can be done to stimulate and help a baby develop his mental processes during the first three months of life. Nothing could be further from the truth. As I have already explained, a new baby is not just a blob of protoplasm whose only requirements are to be fed, changed, and bathed. One look at the growth and development charts brings this point home. New babies can hear, see, and, very early on, react to their surroundings. The key to helping to develop your infant's intellectual capacities during these first three months is to do everything possible to encourage *curiosity.*

### VISUAL SKILLS

You can help your baby develop his visual skills in a number of simple ways.

*Place your baby in the prone position* (on his stomach) a number of times each day. In this position he will be able to raise his head and look around to see more of what is happening around him. If the baby is kept on his back most or all of the time, he will only be able to see what is above him, and in a short time he will become bored and irritable. Even a one-month-old baby thrives on action and activity. Therefore, changing your baby's position and placing him on his stomach makes it easier for him to become involved with his surroundings and with other family members.

*Put your baby in an infant seat* (always remembering to prop him up in order to support his wobbly head). This upright position allows him to look around the room and follow you with his eyes as you go about your daily activities. During his waking hours your infant will not only be happier but will be more stimulated if he is kept near you rather than allowed to remain in the crib.

During the first three months all infants spend a great deal of each day in the crib. Therefore, it is important to *give your baby interesting things to look at while he's in his crib*. It is a good idea to put highly colored pictures on the walls around the crib. Shiny, bright fabric or foil can be hung from the sides of the crib for the first six weeks of life. After that it would be wise to get rid of it, since by then most infants can start to reach. Mobiles can be hung above the crib, but they should always be far enough away so that the baby cannot reach them. Everything a baby grabs goes straight into his mouth.

### HEARING

From the day he is born, a baby hears and absorbs every sound around him; you should always keep this in mind. First and foremost, the tone of your voice should always be soothing and gentle. You will be pleasantly surprised at how responsive your infant will be to happy, cheerful voices and sounds around him. Even the youngest infant seems to enjoy music. You might, therefore, want to have a music box, and also to play music on the radio or from records for your baby's enjoyment. I remember suggesting to a new mother that she sing to her baby. She became upset and I could not understand why. It turned out that her husband made fun of her singing, which he described as being flat and out of tune. It took awhile for me to assure her that her one-month-old was no music critic, and to go right ahead and sing to her heart's content.

To develop your infant's hearing capabilities, you might also attach bells to his bootees. As he kicks, the jingling will please and interest him.

This also helps encourage kicking exercises. Always make certain that the bells are securely attached.

## OTHER SUGGESTIONS

**Crib devices.** These devices, which were discussed in the physical

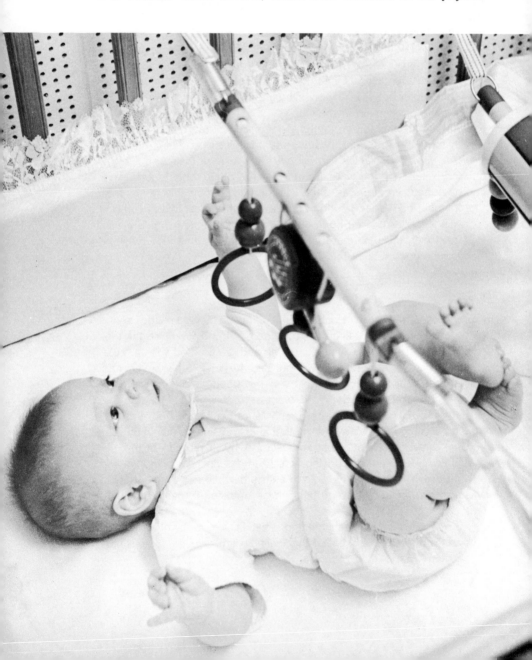

development section of this chapter, are very helpful in stimulating curiosity as well as encouraging physical activity.

**Rattles.** These really are of only limited value for most infants during the first three months. The infant has trouble holding the rattle and will usually drop it quickly and be unable to pick it up. Some infants are more dexterous than others and enjoy holding and shaking a rattle. The important thing to remember is to make sure that any rattles you buy are large and sturdy and nonflammable.

**Repetition.** Babies learn through repetition. Memory is developed through repetitive activities. There is a real question as to the exact age when actual memory begins. Most authorities believe that the start of memory begins at around two and a half to three months of age. It is important and useful for you to give your baby the opportunity to re-peat various actions over and over again. The repetition process should be looked upon as a real learning experience, one which helps your infant develop his intellectual capacities. An example of learning by repetition would be the use of a hanging crib device with bells attached. The baby sees the device and hits or swipes at it. When he makes contact the device moves and the bells ring, and when he misses it nothing happens. As the infant becomes more skillful and dexterous he succeeds more and more often in hitting the device, and his reward for the achievement is seeing the device move and hearing the sound of the ringing bells. The infant remembers what has happened, and this is the start of memory as we know it.

During the first three months an infant must be allowed to have his natural curiosity satisfied. With the few simple devices and activities I have just described, you will help your new baby achieve his maximum mental growth.

# CHAPTER II

# Three to
# Six Months

What can you expect during this period? For one thing, there will be lots of action. Your baby will make some remarkable advances, physically, emotionally, and mentally. Central to these advances will be her ability to learn to deal with things manually. This skill is called *prehension*, the ability to grasp. Between three and six months of age your infant will begin to grasp for what she sees, tastes, or feels. This skill will allow the baby to gradually begin to learn to bring together the spatial information she obtains. The result of the mastering of prehension is that she will be able to coordinate and relate certain of her movements to the environment. This manual dexterity is crucial for her normal development.

Your baby will also begin to develop and master hand/eye coordination. She will now be able to reach for the objects she can clearly see. Further, babies begin to roll over, and some begin to creep. It therefore

25

begins to be possible for the baby to start to explore the world around her.

Let me assure you that during these next three months it will be much easier for you to enjoy your baby and have fun with her than during the first three months. Although she will be awake much more than she was during her first three months of life, she will usually be quite cheerful and happy. It is true that teething may interfere with her usual genial disposition, but aside from the discomfort often associated with the teething process, your baby will be very easy to live with. Recently a mother of a five-month-old girl described her baby as being a "real ham." What she meant was that Yvonne spent most of her waking time performing for her parents in order to attract their attention. Yvonne imitated, babbled, and made all sorts of noises to gain the attention of anybody around her. When her audience responded, Yvonne squealed, chuckled, and kicked her legs in a state of complete euphoria. This description is classic. These three- to six-month-olds really have a happy time of it. They are usually in a pretty good mood even when left alone with their toys. But they almost burst with joy and happiness when the people around them pay attention and respond to their actions. A comedian performing in front of an audience soon becomes discouraged when nobody laughs at his jokes. Your baby is no different. She too will become discouraged and withdrawn if, despite her best efforts, she is not able to get the appropriate response from her family. Her self-esteem gets a big boost when her actions are appreciated and not ignored.

Between three and six months of age you can also expect that your baby will begin to exercise her body and really enjoy doing it. This is an extremely important time in terms of physical development; I will refer back to this later on in the chapter.

A few words about bonding and trust and curiosity. As stated in the previous chapter, the bonding process never stops. It is important that you continue to hold and touch your baby every chance you get. Memory and understanding are developing and your baby is becoming more responsive each day. She depends entirely on you to satisfy all her needs, and if you let her down too often, the trust that must be built up between you will suffer. As your baby grows and develops, she becomes more alert and more curious to explore and learn about her surroundings. I will give you specific recommendations to help you help your baby make the most out of these next three months of her young life after the growth and development charts that follow.

### 3 – 6 Months

## GROWTH AND DEVELOPMENT
*Physical (Motor)*

### 3 – 4 Months

1. May roll from stomach to back.
2. Can sit with propping and support.
3. Reaches with hands more efficiently and purposefully.
4. Swipes at nearby objects, usually successfully.
5. While sitting, holds head fairly steady.
6. While on back, can lift head up.

### 4 – 5 Months

1. On back, lifts up both head and shoulders.
2. Rolls from stomach to back.
3. Sits with support, with head and back steady.
4. May be pulled up to standing position.
5. May be able to hold bottle with both hands or with one.
6. Begins to transfer objects from one hand to another.
7. Starts to reach for and grasp objects.

### 5 – 6 Months

1. On back, can grab feet.
2. Can roll from back to stomach.
3. Sits without much support.
4. Holds bottle well.
5. Begins to reach and swipe with one arm at a time.
6. Starts to learn to manipulate objects in her hands.
7. May grasp small objects off a flat surface.
8. On stomach, starts to creep forward or backward with legs and steer with arms.

*Note:* These charts are based on average *ranges* of growth and development; many normal babies perform and achieve either sooner or later than indicated.

## 3 – 6 Months

## GROWTH AND DEVELOPMENT
*Emotional (Social)*

### 3 – 4 Months

1. Smiles at people easily and openly.
2. Recognizes mother and father.
3. Turns toward familiar voices.
4. Enjoys games and socialization.
5. Laughs loudly, squeals, and chuckles.
6. May coo or sound one syllable; e.g., ooh, ah.
7. May smile at mirror image.

### 4 – 5 Months

1. Recognizes various members of the family.
3. Resists when toy is taken away.
3. Smiles and makes sounds to gain attention.
4. Starts to have angry and fearful reactions.
5. More responsive to human voices; turns and looks at speaker.
6. May start to imitate.
7. Plays with rattles, toys, bottles, etc.

### 5 – 6 Months

1. Can imitate facial expressions and voice inflections.
2. Responds to her name.
3. Smiles at mirror image.
4. Plays games with pleasure and enjoys sound effects; e.g., peek-a-boo.
5. Enjoys other children; smiles and touches them.
6. Makes "raspberry" sound, with tongue between her lips.
7. Disturbed and frightened by strangers.
8. Responds to music with cooing.

*Note:* These charts are based on average *ranges* of growth and development; many normal babies perform and achieve either sooner or later than indicated.

## 3 – 6 Months

## GROWTH AND DEVELOPMENT
*Mental (Intellectual)*

### 3 — 4 Months

1. Alert and responsive to surroundings and people around her.
2. Reaches for toys that are out of reach.
3. Memory span increasing to up to 10 seconds.
4. Recognizes various members of her family.
5. Aware of her hands, and carries objects to her mouth.

### 4 — 5 Months

1. Awake and alert for longer periods of time.
2. Looks down for falling objects.
3. Imitates sounds and movements.
4. Fearful of strangers and new situations.
5. Recognizes familiar objects and people, and reacts appropriately.
6. May say vowel sounds and some consonants: b, d, m.
7. Memory span continues to increase.

### 5 — 6 Months

1. Starts to reach for dropped toys.
2. May begin to compare two objects at a time.
3. Uses her fingers and mouth to explore objects around her.
4. Can lift a cup by its handle.
5. Can reach for and grasp the things she sees.
6. Stares and studies objects carefully and for long periods of time.
7. Says many consonants and vowels.

*Note:* These charts are based on average *ranges* of growth and development; many normal babies perform and achieve either sooner or later than indicated.

## PHYSICAL (MOTOR) DEVELOPMENT

### NUTRITION

The main source of nourishment for your baby between three and six months of age should continue to be breast milk or commercially-prepared formula. As stated in the previous chapter, there is general agreement among pediatricians that breast feeding is the ideal way to feed a baby. If you have chosen to breast feed your baby, I would encourage you to continue to do so during these next three months if you possibly can. As a matter of fact, the longer you are able to breast feed, the better off your baby will be. If, for whatever reason, you decide to discontinue breast feeding your baby any time during these three months, it is most important that you switch to formula and *not* to cow's milk. As noted earlier, commercial formulas are specifically designed to meet all the nutritional needs of the infant and so are very close to breast milk in their nutrient mix. Cow's milk may be ideal for baby cows, but it never was designed for human babies. More and more evidence has accumulated pointing to the potential dangers of feeding cow's milk to infants who are under six months of age.

Cow's milk contains too much salt and too much protein, much more than in either breast milk or commercially prepared formula. This excessive quantity of salt and protein can place added strain on the infant's kidneys. The kidneys must work harder in order to eliminate the extra salt and protein, and they use up a great deal of water in the process. If a baby drinking cow's milk develops diarrhea which results in her losing large amounts of water, she will become dehydrated and get into real trouble much more rapidly than the infant with diarrhea who is being breast fed or who is taking formula. There is yet another problem with feeding a baby cow's milk at this age. A certain percentage of infants who drink cow's milk bleed a little bit in their gastrointestinal tracts; this is thought to be caused by the protein in the cow's milk. This bleeding can lead to iron-deficiency anemia. Despite all these known potential dangers it has been my experience that many mothers still switch to cow's milk before the baby is six months of age. This is certainly not the ideal way to feed your baby, and I would strongly recommend that you not do so.

If your baby has been fed formula during her first three months, my advice is the same. Continue to use formula; do not change over to cow's milk. I am often asked about the total quantity of formula an infant should be permitted to consume during each twenty-four-hour period. I can't give you a direct answer to the question because of infants' variable energy requirements. What I can say is that if you allow your infant to stop each feeding at the first sign of satiation or of willingness to stop, it is highly unlikely that she will ever be over- or underfed. As a general rule, after three months of age very few infants consume more than two and a half ounces per pound per day. For example, a baby weighing twelve pounds will probably not drink more than a total of thirty ounces of formula each day. If your infant has a voracious appetite and is gaining weight too rapidly by drinking tremendous amounts of formula, the simplest way to slow down the monthly weight gain is to dilute the formula with some water. Before doing so, I would suggest that you discuss it with your baby's physician.

What about the introduction of solid foods? A number of surveys have shown that most infants in the United States today are fed some solid food or other well before they are two months of age. My experience confirms these findings. All the authorities in the field agree that this is much too early for solid foods. The two main reasons for the too-early introduction of "beikost" (meaning foods other than milk or formula fed to infants) are the belief that they will help the baby sleep through the night (a myth dispelled in the previous chapter), and outside social pressures. Too many mothers seem to compete with each other to see who can feed solids to her baby earlier. I am very upset when I hear parents brag about all the solid food they push down their infant's throat long before the baby requires any at all. We have already stated some of the reasons for not starting solids too early; namely, unnecessary extra calories, and the potential for developing allergies later on. Another important reason for not rushing to give your infant solid foods is that doing so can interfere with the establishment of proper eating habits. Since it is important that an infant be encouraged to stop eating when satisfied, she must be able to communicate this feeling to the person who is feeding her. At four to five months of age, most infants can sit with support and have relatively good control of their heads and necks. These babies are able to lean forward and open their mouths when interested in the food, and are also able to lean backwards and turn away when not interested or satiated. If solid foods are introduced before the age of four months, the infant will find it difficult to make her feelings known, and this will result in forced feedings. The key to proper feeding is to allow your baby to decide when the feeding is over, and not to stop the feeding when *you* think she's had enough. This simple concept will do much to establish correct feeding habits — and these habits will continue as the child grows and develops. They will go a long way to ensure your child a full, active, and healthy future.

It usually takes a few days' practice for your infant to learn to swallow from a spoon. I would suggest that you start with just one teaspoon of solid food the first day and gradually increase the quantity each day.

It would be prudent to start only one new food at a time, and give each for a few days, in order to be sure that the baby can tolerate what she is fed. The signs of food intolerance or allergy are vomiting, gassiness, rashes, and excessive crankiness. If any of these signs develop, simply stop that particular food and go on to another kind.

The sequence I follow for the introduction of solids varies, of course, from baby to baby. A number of different factors need to be taken into consideration. Your baby's doctor is in the best position to decide when and what foods to give. The following is the average schedule of solid foods recommended to my patients for the three- to six-month period:

| Age | Type of solid food | Time |
| --- | --- | --- |
| 3 months | None | |
| 4 months | Precooked cereals 2 times a day | Morning and evening |
| 5 months | Add strained single fruits 2 times a day | Morning and evening |
| 6 months | Add strained vegetables | Lunch |

Cereals are mixed with formula. Fruits and vegetables are fed without adding formula. Always feed with a spoon. It is not a good idea to add any solid food to the bottle.

Infant cereals are introduced first because they all are fortified with iron in a form that is easily and readily absorbed. Breast-fed babies require extra iron at around four to five months of age, as do infants fed formulas that are not iron-fortified. By this age, most infants have pretty well depleted the iron supplies they received at birth from their mothers. If iron is not introduced into their diets at this time, there is a good chance that they will be started on the road to iron-deficiency anemia. Studies have shown that an infant who is allowed to develop severe iron deficiency that is not corrected over a long period of time has a greater risk of developing learning disabilities later on in life. If your baby is not fed cereal at this age, iron should be supplied by giving one of the iron drop preparations or an iron-fortified multivitamin drop preparation. Babies who are fed an iron-fortified formula are protected against iron deficiency and so do not require another source of iron at this age.

This is a good time to discuss sugar and salt. It is unhealthy for a baby (and for anybody, for that matter) to eat too much salt. Whether you make your own baby foods with a blender or use commercial products, do not add sugar or salt. The baby food manufacturers have recently removed added salt from all their products, and added sugar from most, and what remains is the natural-occurring salt and sugar. This is an important forward step in fostering proper nutrition. You should not allow your baby to become accustomed to foods that are either too salty or too sweet. Food tastes and preferences are established early in life. No baby is born a "sugar freak" or a salt craver. Foods contain enough natural salt and sugar to take care of all your baby's nutritional needs. Eliminating extra salt and sugar from your baby's diet can help prevent the later development of high blood pressure, dental decay, and obesity.

EXERCISE

Your three- to six-month-old baby loves to exercise. My best advice is to give her the space and allow her to do as much exercising as possible. You do not need to buy any fancy equipment for this purpose. The following are my recommendations for exercising a three- to six-month-old baby:

**Crib devices.** These have already been described in Chapter I. Suffice it to say that now your baby can start to grasp and reach and is becoming increasingly proficient at these activities. She will make excellent use of the device attached to her crib, and this is a good form of physical activity.

**Don't swaddle your baby by wrapping her tightly in clothing and blankets.** I am totally opposed to this practice. Your baby should be given the freedom to move her arms and kick her legs freely, without restraint.

**Turn-over games.** Babies never seem to get tired of or bored with turning over again and again and again. This activity is great fun for the baby and is an excellent exercise as well. It does much to tone up the muscles and to increase her agility. Although you may get tired of watching her, your baby won't tire of doing it, so give her every opportunity to practice — and react appropriately when she succeeds.

**Kicking toys.** You can either buy or make your own large cuddly kicking toy and attach it to the sides of the crib. These kicking toys can be a continuing source of pleasure for your baby as she kicks at them and also grabs for them. These not only keep her busy and happy but also allow her to develop strength in her legs.

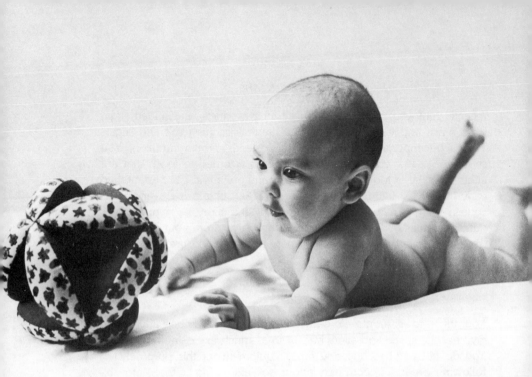

***Creeping and rocking along.*** Many five- to six-month-old babies start to creep or push themselves along, either forward or backward. It therefore makes good sense to take your baby out of the crib a number of times each day. Either put the baby on the floor (clear of small and sharp objects) or in a playpen so that she can have the space to practice and develop these new skills. Starting to get from one place to another in order to explore her environment is an exciting time for your baby and you should encourage this form of exercise as much as possible.

***Standing.*** Sometime between three and six months of age most babies can support their weight while standing supported. Get your baby up on her feet. This will help her develop strength in her lower extremities as well as improve her large-muscle coordination.

As I noted earlier, standing a baby too early will not cause bowlegs. There is absolutely no truth to this old wives' tale. I am often asked by parents about how long to stand a baby up. My answer is, just as long as the baby is happy doing it.

The important thing to remember is that exercise habits start early in life. The infant who is kept swaddled and restricted, is not permitted to begin to explore her environment, and is discouraged from exercising every step of the way, will very soon become discouraged and inactive.

If your goal is optimal physical development, you should encourage your baby to use all her muscles. At this age it is not difficult to give her all the exercising she wants and needs.

***Never leave your baby alone on any elevated surface.*** Three- to six-month-olds can turn over, and some can creep and move around, so you are really looking for trouble if you leave them unattended. A sensible idea is to use a safety strap.

**Smothering.** Plastic bags, long toy telephone cords, harnesses, and soft pillows all can smother or strangle a baby. Obviously, all these should always be kept away from your baby. A firm crib mattress and loose covering for the sleeping baby are safest.

**Small and sharp objects.** It is important to keep pills, buttons, pins, beads, and any other small or sharp objects away from your baby's reach. At this age everything goes into the mouth. I will never forget making a house call and finding the five-month-old sick baby lying on her dressing table, securely strapped down. As I started to examine her mouth, I was horrified to see an open safety pin already halfway down her throat. Fortunately, I was able to grab it and pull it out before it disappeared from view. I am not sure who was more upset about this incident, the mother or me.

**Burns.** Always check the bath water temperature first, in order to prevent scalding your baby. Never drink hot liquids such as coffee or tea while holding your baby on your lap.

**Immunizations.** I include these here because it is unsafe for your baby not to be immunized in time. Many parents have been lulled into a false sense of security because of the widespread immunization programs of recent years. However, I want to remind you that it is extremely important that you arrange for your infant to receive all the immunizations she requires — and the sooner you get started, the better. The sad facts are that currently over five million children, ages one to four, are unprotected against polio, measles, mumps, rubella (German measles), whooping cough, diphtheria, or tetanus. This is a national disgrace. Unfortunately, many parents wait until their child is ready to start school before giving them immunizations. Therefore, a large number of children are unprotected during the first few years of life, which is just the period when they are most vulnerable to many of these dangerous illnesses. Further, the effects of many of these diseases are most serious during the first few months of life, when the infant's central nervous system is most susceptible. A large segment of our population does not realize that these diseases are not just harmless childhood illnesses. All of them can either cripple or kill a child, and all are preventable by immunization.

Most physicians treating children routinely start to immunize them when the infant is two to three months of age. By age two years, all children should be fully immunized against polio, whooping cough, diphtheria, tetanus, measles, mumps, and rubella (German measles). It

is your responsibility to make certain that this is accomplished. A child whose brain is damaged from measles encephalitis or who is paralyzed from polio cannot grow up to achieve her maximum potential. If you conclude from what I have written that I am using scare tactics, you are right. I have seen too many preventable tragedies through the years because children, for whatever reason, have not received their immunizations. They are safe, effective, and readily available, so there is no excuse for neglecting or postponing them.

**Hearing.** The following may be danger signals pointing to hearing difficulties during this period. If you notice either one, tell your infant's doctor about it.

1. Your four-month-old does not turn to the source of a distant sound.
2. Your six-month-old gradually stops her babbling noises.

## EMOTIONAL (SOCIAL) DEVELOPMENT

We are back to bonding and trust. During this period in your infant's life it becomes much easier for you to relate in a positive way. Since three- to six-month-old babies are so alert, cheerful, and responsive, you should find each day interesting, different, and a real adventure. The bonding process that started the moment your baby was born continues. For the emotional well-being of your baby this positive nurturing relationship between the baby and her parents must be reinforced and solidified every single day.

The actual number of hours you spend with your baby is not as important as how you spend each hour. In discussing this with parents I often use the term "quality time." Just being around and not relating or responding to all your baby's needs is not what quality or positive parenting is all about. I also do not mean just responding when your baby cries. When she is cooing or gurgling or laughing, she also is communicating her feelings to you, and you should respond in kind. Show affection by holding, kissing, cuddling, and talking to her in a soothing, loving voice. Your little baby understands exactly what you are trying to get across to her. All your baby needs is your love, so why skimp on it or ration it out?

Parents often ask me if there is any way they can determine if they are, in fact, giving their baby enough love and affection. Since there is no way to measure these, there is no real answer to their question. All I can say is that mothers and fathers who are thinking about this aspect of parenting are on the right track and most probably are satisfying their baby's emotional needs.

**Myth:** *A baby who is frightened by strangers is insecure and unloved!* Absolutely not. Somewhere between four and six months of age, some babies develop a fear of strangers. This can be considered normal behavior. The fear disappears in time and is nothing to be concerned about. This brings to mind a recent experience in my practice. Baby Elizabeth, age five months, was upsetting her parents enough that they brought her to my office to find out if there was anything wrong. It seems that Elizabeth, a happy, healthy, and friendly baby, screamed with fright everytime Grandma came to visit and picked her up. It took me quite awhile to convince the family, including Grandma, who also came along, that Elizabeth was perfect in every way, and that there was no reason to worry. Incidentally, by the time Elizabeth was nine months old her favorite visitor was Grandma.

During this period your infant wants very much to keep everybody around her amused. She turns and kicks and reaches, and she laughs and giggles and coos. She deserves to have her performance appreciated, especially by the people closest to her. I once got a 10:00 P.M. phone call from the mother of a five-and-a-half-month-old baby. She was bursting with pride and happiness as she told me what had just happened. While changing the baby's diaper Mrs. T. suddenly sneezed. Baby Emily gave out a big belly laugh in response to the sneeze, and both mother and baby then had a mutual laughing session. Momma actually could not wait to share this happy experience with her pediatrician. I was quite happy hearing the story, but I was even happier that Mrs. T. hadn't sneezed at 3:00 A.M.!

### GAMES

There are some simple games that you can play with a three- to six-month-old, games that your infant not only will enjoy but that will also increase the bonding and trust that are so essential for a baby's emotional well-being:

**Peek-a-boo-games.** Make them up as you go along; they all work fine.

**Tickling games.** Baby loves to be tickled at this age, and giggle and laugh in response.

**Drop-the-spoon games.** Usually by five to six months of age infants learn to reach for dropped objects. They also enjoy having you pick up the spoon, and can't wait to drop it again. This is great fun for them, but sometimes not such great fun for your aching back.

*This little piggy went to market.* Wiggle each of her toes as you say the lines.

*Making faces.* Infants at this stage are learning to imitate, and have a marvelous time doing so.

Many parents do not realize how important it is for them to regularly play with their babies. I have mentioned previously and will continue to repeat that feeding, changing, and bathing are not enough. Your baby deserves more out of life than that, and it is so very easy for you to give it to her. Sharing fun games together is a must.

Infants are very attuned to their surroundings. Emotional stability is nurtured by friendly, familiar, affectionate voices, laughter, and singing. Babies also require and respond to close physical contact. There is no such thing as too much touching, holding, and carrying around.

**Myth:** *A baby is spoiled by "too much attention."* In my opinion, just the opposite is true.

## MENTAL (INTELLECTUAL) DEVELOPMENT

Sometime between three and six months of age your baby will begin to show signs of intelligence as we usually understand it. The question as to the actual age intelligence develops is a favorite of infant developmental psychologists. I would say that intelligence begins on the day of birth. Nevertheless, the usual signs that we associate with intelligence become obvious between three and six months of age. The infant now learns to use her hand as a reaching tool under the guidance and direction of her eyes. Your little baby will now simultaneously see, reach, and touch. Besides this establishment of efficient hand/eye coordination, your baby will now show real interest in the objects she can reach, and so it makes good sense to give her as many interesting objects as possible to look at, feel, and handle.

### SPECIFIC RECOMMENDATIONS

The following are some specific recommendations for stimulating your infant to develop her intellectual capacities to the fullest between three and six months of age.

**Use an infant seat.** Move the location of the infant seat frequently so as to change your baby's environment. Try to keep her near you in her infant seat as you go about doing your chores. Keeping her close to you rather than isolated in another room not only will result in her being happy and pleased to have your company, but at the same time it will open up many new opportunities for learning.

**Take your baby outside.** Frequent walks in the carriage will do both you and your baby a lot of good. This will encourage and stimulate her interest in the outside world. The more she sees and the more she is exposed to, the better.

   **Myth:** *Babies catch cold if taken outdoors during cold weather in the winter.* This is ridiculous. Colds are caused by a number of different viruses, and babies catch cold from being exposed to another person who is carrying a particular cold virus. These upper respiratory infections have nothing to do with the temperature outside. As a matter of fact it has been my experience that infants who are taken out into the fresh air are healthier as a group than the ones who are cooped up inside most of the time.

**Talk to your baby.** You may think it strange that I suggest talking to your baby, since it is so obvious. Let me assure you that many parents simply do not realize how crucial it is for them to talk to their infants at this age. They wrongly assume that since the baby cannot understand the actual meaning of the words, they should not bother. The beginning of language learning starts during this three-month period. If you talk to your baby about what is taking place around her, development of the language-learning process will be stimulated. Many studies have demonstrated significant differences in intelligence later on in life between those infants who were largely deprived of language interchange and those who were spoken to on a regular basis.

**Set up mobiles and mirrors.** These should be placed over the crib, but far enough away from the baby that she cannot actually reach out and grab them. They can be quite interesting to the infant and serve as another source of learning. Babies at this age enjoy looking at themselves in the mirror and watching the mobiles move around above them. It gets pretty boring being incarcerated in a crib with nothing much to do or to look at.

**Using a playpen.** There are differences of opinion regarding the usefulness of playpens at this age. I think they are quite useful. While in a playpen your baby is safe, and you do not have to watch continually over her, as you would if she were allowed to play on the floor. Her playpen should be stocked with interesting, safe objects such as rattles, plastic balls and containers, spoons, and lids of pots. Banging pots and pans seems to be one activity that almost all babies enjoy. Clutch balls and squeaky toys also should be provided. Supplying your infant with a variety of these objects allows her to play by herself for long periods of time without becoming bored. They also give her the opportunity to learn more rapidly.

These same objects can obviously also be used while your baby is in her crib.

*Imitation.* This is an important mental skill which usually starts at around five months of age or earlier. The infant begins to imitate various signs and movements, and this should be encouraged by you. The first step in imitation learning is for you to copy the things the baby does. In short order she will begin to understand what you are doing and will start to do her own imitating.

*Sounds and voices.* Let your baby hear as many different sounds as possible, such as a clock ticking, the vacuum cleaner, music, the radio, and so on. Give her the opportunity of hearing not only your voice but the sounds you are making as you move about and work in the house. This can only be done if you keep her near you as much of the time as possible.

Your baby is eager to learn and to explore her environment. It is very easy for you to help her attain maximum intellectual development during this period. You need no expensive or elaborate equipment. It just takes the few suggestions I have outlined. The extra time this requires of you is well worth your effort.

# CHAPTER III

# Six to Nine Months

## INTRODUCTION

This period in your baby's life has been aptly called the early exploratory stage. By this time he has developed many of the skills that make it possible to interact with and explore the world around him. As the growth and development charts that follow indicate, he will now be able to reach efficiently for and grasp objects, even very tiny ones. Babies at this stage have excellent control of their hands and are fascinated with manipulating the various objects they can grab. In addition, a baby's eyes and ears now function very effectively. He can focus well on objects near and far, and can localize sounds without difficulty. He is able to maintain excellent head control and can freely move his head around in all directions. He will be spending more and more time in the sitting

position and so will be able to see much more of what is going on around him. During these three months most babies learn to crawl or drag themselves along the floor, and some learn to stand and "cruise" along the furniture. It therefore becomes possible for these babies to start to travel and to investigate what is happening some distance away.

As he becomes more and more proficient in turning, crawling, creeping, kicking, and standing, a six- to nine-month-old is even more involved in physical activity than when he was younger. His interest in games increases day by day. A favorite pastime is to drop objects and to watch and wait to see what happens next. It is amazing how well he is now able to concentrate on a particular activity. By repeating the same task over and over again, he finally learns to master it, and remembers what he has done. I recall talking to the father of a seven-month-old boy. He could not believe that Johnny never seemed to tire of turning over and over and over again. Further, this little fellow took pride and satisfaction in this accomplishment every single time. It is important to always remember that learning a new skill takes a lot of practice, and an appreciative audience speeds up the process.

This is a period in your baby's life when he develops a tremendous amount of curiosity. He will want to touch and feel and taste everything he can find and hold. It is essential that you encourage him and give him the opportunity to expand his skills and his horizons. A couple of years ago the mother of an extremely active and adventurous eight-month-old bitterly complained to me that she was sure that Danny was born "bad." I sat her down in my consultation room and asked her why she felt that way. "Dr. Eden, he is a devil. He gets into trouble all the time just to make my life miserable. He crawls around and puts everything in his mouth. Would you believe that yesterday he actually pulled an electric plug out of the wall and tried to put it in his mouth?" It took me fully thirty minutes to convince her that Danny was not "bad" but rather was an intelligent, healthy, and curious young man and that she should thank God that she had such a fine, brave youngster. I also spent a few minutes gently suggesting some simple safety measures that she had better adopt if she wanted to avoid a serious accident.

Teeth are coming in at this time, and some babies suffer more discomfort from it than others. Despite the fussiness and crankiness that often accompanies teething, babies during these three months basically are cheerful and contented. They try to be social and appreciate plenty of attention and activity. They smile, giggle, and laugh a lot, and it doesn't take much to get them into a good mood.

**Myth:** *Teething causes high fever.* Not true. If your baby has a temperature of over 101°F. it is *not* due to teething.

Despite the fact that your baby is beginning to be able to move around, he will still be confined most of the time to his crib, playpen, or infant seat. It is interesting that he usually does not seem to mind being a prisoner. This is especially true when he is around six to seven months old. By eight to nine months of age he may not be too happy if he is prevented from moving freely about the room. He then will begin to show signs of frustration when not allowed to initiate various explorations and expeditions.

Memory and understanding develop rapidly, day by day. Ideas are beginning to take shape in his busy, active mind. Verbal understanding is starting. He will learn to understand the meaning of some words such as mama, dada, bye-bye. It will be a happy day indeed when he is able to follow the first instructions you give him such as to wave bye-bye. Most babies achieve this milestone sometime during these fascinating three months.

## 6 – 9 Months

## GROWTH AND DEVELOPMENT
*Physical (Motor)*

### 6 – 7 Months

1. Sits well with little support.
2. Can grasp with thumb and fingers.
3. Creeps and then starts to crawl.
4. Turns, back to stomach and stomach to back.
5. Stands with support.
6. Holds and handles spoon and cup.
7. Gets himself into sitting position in crib or on floor.

### 7 – 8 Months

1. Sits without support.
2. Crawls, forward or backward.
3. Stands well with support.
4. Skillfully picks up small objects, using "pincer" grasp (thumb and forefinger).
5. Pulls himself up to standing position, using furniture to help.
6. Once standing, usually cannot get back down.
7. Can feed himself cracker.

### 8 – 9 Months

1. Sits well in chair without support for long periods.
2. Crawls efficiently, even with one hand holding a toy.
3. Starts to "cruise" along furniture.
4. Can crawl upstairs.
5. Manipulates one object in each hand.
6. May stand alone for a moment.
7. Can pull himself up to a standing position, often in the middle of the night; calls for help to get back down.

*Note:* These charts are based on average *ranges* of growth and development; many normal babies perform and achieve either sooner or later than indicated.

## 6 – 9 Months

### GROWTH AND DEVELOPMENT
*Emotional (Social)*

### 6 – 7 Months

1. Often afraid of strangers.
2. Start of sense of humor and teasing behavior.
3. Understands different tones of voice and meaning of "no."
4. Happy to play with toys.
5. Also wants to be included in games such as pat-a-cake, and in social interaction.

### 7 – 8 Months

1. Still afraid of strangers.
2. Attached to mother or primary caretaker and fears separation.
3. Demands and shouts for attention.
4. Longer attention span and sustained interest in play.
5. Pats at and kisses mirror image.
6. Upset when confined.

### 8 – 9 Months

1. Enjoys being center of attention.
2. Eager for approval, and imitates play.
3. Pleased with audience response to his exploits.
4. Selective in the toys he plays with.
5. Loves various games, with dolls and blocks, pat-a-cake, peek-a-boo, etc.
6. May start to show signs of selfish behavior; e.g., protects his toys.

*Note:* These charts are based on average *ranges* of growth and development; many normal babies perform and achieve either sooner or later than indicated.

## 6 – 9 Months

GROWTH AND DEVELOPMENT
*Mental (Intellectual)*

### 6 — 7 Months

1. Can distinguish distances, near and far.
2. Starts to learn to understand the implications and consequences of his actions and behavior.
3. May say "mama" and "dada" without attaching meaning to them.
4. Imitates the speech sounds he hears.
5. Memory improving; responds with excitement to repetition of event.

### 7 — 8 Months

1. Can solve simple problems.
2. Starts to understand the meaning of a few words, such as his name, bottle, mama.
3. Good memory of recent events.
4. Says a few words, still without knowing their meaning, sometimes in two syllables.
5. Imitates people and behavior; e.g., waving bye-bye, and clapping and pointing to and following what someone else points to.

### 8 — 9 Months

1. Follows simple instructions.
2. Learns to build two-block tower.
3. Understands cause and effect.
4. May be able to keep a series of ideas in mind, as memory and thinking processes improve.
5. Becomes bored more easily with repetition of same games and activities.
6. Understands concept of reward.

*Note:* These charts are based on average *ranges* of growth and development; many normal babies perform and achieve either sooner or later than indicated.

## PHYSICAL (MOTOR) DEVELOPMENT

### NUTRITION

It has been my experience that many mothers who have breast fed their babies stop by the time the infant is six months of age. But, unless there is a specific reason to stop, I would advise that breast feeding be continued during this six- to nine-month period. Throughout human history the weaning age has been well over one year, often somewhere between two and three years. There is certainly no reason to stop breast feeding when your baby is six months old. It would be best to continue to breast feed if at all possible. This leads me to the problem of the mother who chooses, for whatever reason, to go back to work during this period or even earlier. There is little question that a full-time job creates problems for the breast-feeding mother. One sensible solution is to use a formula for the one or two feedings the mother is away from her home and to continue to breast feed the remainder of the time. In this way many mothers successfully continue to breast feed while doing a full day's work outside the house. I will be discussing the working mother in greater detail in a subsequent chapter (Twelve to Eighteen Months).

Babies who have been fed one of the commercially prepared formulas should *remain* on the formula and should not be switched to whole cow's milk during this three-month period. I agree with the Committee of Nutrition of the American Academy of Pediatrics, who recently recommended this too. My reasons for avoiding cow's milk between six and nine months of age are the same as those I previously discussed; namely, that there is too much protein and too much salt in cow's milk for the baby's kidneys. You probably no longer need to worry about intestinal bleeding due to cow's milk. The reports implicating cow's milk as a cause of gastrointestinal bleeding have primarily involved infants below six months of age. Some authorities on infant nutrition take the position that if a baby over six months of age is eating the daily equivalent of about one and a half jars of commercially prepared strained food, there should be no objection to starting him on whole cow's milk. Their rationale is that most beikost items are rich in carbohydrates, while whole milk is rich in protein and fat, and so the combination is well balanced nutritionally. My position is that although cow's milk is probably safe for a baby over six months of age, it is sounder feeding practice to extend the use of formula and not take any chances. It is also a good idea to limit the total amount of formula per day to under one quart. If your baby is consuming much over a quart per day, and especially if he is gaining weight too rapidly, a simple solution is to dilute the formula with some water. For example, each eight-ounce bottle can be made up of six ounces of formula mixed with two ounces of water.

Skim milk should *never* be used at this age. Parents have recently become more concerned about childhood obesity and assume that using skim milk makes sense (as is the case in treating adult obesity). The fact is that there is even more salt in skim milk than in regular cow's milk. Furthermore, many studies have shown that skim milk does not satisfy the energy requirements of infants. It has no place in the diet of any baby during the first year of life.

More and more of the total infant diet will now be made up of beikost (solid foods). The order in which you introduce various solid foods really makes little difference. But what is important is to continue to feed your baby infant cereals which, as you will recall, are all iron-fortified and so extremely important in preventing the development of iron-deficiency anemia. Unfortunately, I see many parents starting their six- to nine-month-old babies on a variety of other cereals that are not specifically prepared for infants. Although many of these may be iron fortified, a good number have iron in a form that is not readily bioavailable and thus is poorly absorbed by the baby. For this reason I would strongly recommend that you continue to feed your baby infant cereals until he is eighteen months of age in order to supply him with sufficient iron during the period in his life when he is most susceptible to iron-deficiency.

For this six- to nine-month age period, the following are my recommendations for additional solid foods:

| Age | Type of solid food | Time |
|---|---|---|
| 6 – 7 months | Plain yogurt | Snack |
| | Strained meats | Lunch |
| 7 – 8 months | Egg yolk (strained, commercial or home cooked) | Morning (every other day) |
| 8 – 9 months | Baby juices (no sugar added) | Afternoon |

You will note in the above table that I suggest giving egg yolk only every other day. There is a good reason for this. Eggs certainly are an excellent food nutritionally, but they are also very rich in cholesterol. As adults we are told that we should not eat more than three or four eggs per week in order to reduce our cholesterol intake. It therefore follows that since eating habits and patterns are established early in life, why not also get the baby accustomed to eating an egg only every other day? In subsequent chapters I will be discussing the whole question of cholesterol in greater detail.

I have included plain yogurt in the table because I believe that it is an excellent food to introduce early into your baby's diet. Yogurt is a milk product and so should be considered a substitute for some of the breast milk or formula rather than as part of the solid food diet. I consider yogurt good for babies for the following reasons:

1. It is well tolerated and easily digested.
2. Its consistency makes it easy for the baby to swallow.
3. For adults, yogurt tends to be filling and satisfying, and there is no reason to believe that the same does not hold true for babies.
4. Yogurt is a nutritious, natural product that is high in protein and relatively low in calories.
5. For those babies who cut down on their total daily milk intake, yogurt is an excellent substitute.
6. Acquiring a taste for plain yogurt in infancy will make it more likely that your baby will continue to eat and enjoy it as he grows up.
7. Eating yogurt as a snack food throughout childhood is far healthier and more nutritionally sound than eating so-called "junk" foods, which are less nutritious and too high in refined sugar and calories.

Along with the additional foods I have listed in the table above, your baby can now also be started on desserts, teething crackers, and various baby "dinners." These are lumpier in consistency than strained foods and prepare the baby for regular table foods.

At around seven to eight months of age, "finger" foods may be started, such as zweiback, teething biscuits, and pieces of banana. By the time they are nine months old, many babies become adept at handling pieces of cheese or a slice of apple. There is little question that these finger foods do not help to maintain the cleanliness of the room where your baby is eating, but they do give him some necessary practice in using his fingers and also in spoon-feeding himself, which usually starts later. Further, babies at this age like to feel the various foods they eat and so they should be given that opportunity.

Fruit juices are now being introduced, so a word of caution about so-called "nursing bottle caries" is due. It has been shown that babies who use the bottle as a pacifier, and suck on the bottle containing juice (or milk, for that matter) while lying down for extended periods of time, destroy their teeth. Because of this, some pediatricians recommend that fruit juice should only be fed by cup. I see no reason not to give your baby juice in a bottle. The important thing to remember is that he should drink it only while in an upright position. If your baby must have a bottle in order to fall asleep, make sure it contains only water. This approach will not only save your baby's teeth, but will also save you a lot in dental bills.

Before completing this discussion on nutrition I want to remind you again about obesity. The facts are very clear. Fat babies have a better chance of ending up fat adults than do normal-weight or thin babies. If you notice that your baby has been gaining weight with great rapidity, it is important that you talk this over with his doctor. There are a number of ways of determining if a baby is fat. These include weight charts and the actual measurement of skin folds with special calipers. As far as I am concerned, the best method of all is the "eyeball" test. Just look at him. If he looks fat, he is fat. It is pretty hard not to notice the rolls of fat and extra chins. One rule of thumb you might find useful is that normally a baby should have doubled his birth weight by five months of age. For example, a baby with a birth weight of seven pounds should weigh around fourteen pounds by the time he is five months old. Thus, if your six-month-old weighs considerably more than double his original birth weight, be on the alert. You should also be aware of another important factor related to obesity. Obesity runs in families. The statistics are as follows: If both parents are fat, there is an 80 percent chance that their baby will be fat. If one parent is obese, the baby has a 50 percent chance of being fat, and if both parents are thin, he has only a 10 percent chance. The message from this is clear. If you and/or your spouse is fat, you must be especially careful *never* to allow your baby to gain weight too rapidly. This brings to mind an interesting case. A couple brought their nine-month-old girl to my office for the first time for a checkup. The baby was tremendously overweight, but surprisingly, both her parents were quite slim. Neither the mother nor father was aware of or particularly interested in the fact that Amanda was so fat. I also was not overly concerned since she was lucky enough to have two thin parents, so that her chance of remaining fat was relatively small. As I took her history from the parents, I quickly learned that Amanda was adopted and they had no information about the weight of her natural parents! Genetics went out the window and we got busy discussing the

dangers of childhood obesity. Amanda's diet was adjusted and her opportunities for exercising increased. I am happy to report that now, at around three years of age, Amanda is probably thin enough to pass the "eyeball" test of any neutral observer.

### EXERCISE

The motor growth and development chart should make it obvious that your baby is now really ready for a good deal of physical activity. He is able to sit well, is beginning to stand, can pull himself up to a standing position, crawls and creeps, and may even begin to "cruise" along the furniture. He is now able to turn efficiently, both from front to back and back to front, and can pull himself along the ground on his hands and knees.

In my opinion these six- to nine-month-olds do not require any particular specific exercise program. It is not necessary to buy any special exercise equipment. All your baby needs is the *space* to move around; he will do the rest. Since he can now crawl he will not always be very happy sitting in an infant seat or confined to his playpen. He requires wide open spaces — to crawl, creep, pivot around, rock along, and cruise. Since he is so full of curiosity, he will want to reach every corner of every room, studying everything in sight and trying to put everything he can grab hold of into his mouth. Very few infants at this age need to be encouraged to move around. All you have to do is give them the freedom and opportunity to do so. The only exception is the baby who is markedly overweight. A very obese baby is often content with merely sitting or lying down, preferably with a bottle of milk or juice or a snack of finger food to keep him occupied. A vicious cycle is set up. The fatter the baby, the less active he becomes; and the less active the baby, the fewer calories he burns up, which causes him to become even fatter. Most of his caloric expenditure seems to be the result of chewing and sucking, and this type of exercise burns up very few calories indeed.

I am often asked about the usefulness of walkers for the six- to nine-month-old. The truth of the matter is that I have no strong feelings either way. I don't believe that walkers are essential, but on the other hand, if your baby enjoys using one, by all means let him.

Some babies enjoy a walker, and when using it, are able to rapidly travel long distances. The use of a walker helps them explore so they can satisfy their curiosity; it is also excellent for strengthening their leg muscles. The other side of the coin is that if your baby uses his walker a great deal of the time, it may slow him down both in learning to balance himself on his feet and in learning to walk. Since he can get around so well in the walker, he may be less interested and less motivated to practice walking by himself.

If you do use a walker for your baby, it is important to be careful about possible accidents. The areas in which he may maneuver with his walker must be cleared of anything dangerous. Another point to remember regarding safety is that a baby in a walker has both hands free for getting into trouble. A baby who cruises around on his own uses one hand for support and has only one hand free to grab what may be the wrong object. If you decide to use a walker, make certain that it is well constructed, sturdy, and stable. I have seen too many accidents resulting from faulty construction of a walker (see the section on Safety Tips).

Babies at this age are full of life and full of fun and very anxious to be physically handled. They love to be swung up in the air, bounced up and down on your knee, and are positively ecstatic when their mother or father gets down on the floor with them for some physical tussling and communal crawling. All these activities promote physical vigor, coordination, and agility, and also help to burn up extra calories. Equally important is the fact that promoting and encouraging physical activity at this early age will make it much more likely that your baby will continue to practice and enjoy vigorous physical pursuits throughout his entire childhood and beyond. This will do much to help keep him healthy and happy throughout his life.

I should like to call your attention to one common mistake many parents make at around this age, and that is buying a pair of walking shoes just as soon as the baby is able to stand.

**Myth:** *Shoes make it easier for the baby to walk.* As a matter of fact, just the opposite is true. A baby will learn to walk sooner and better if he is allowed to feel the ground underneath him with his feet unencumbered by shoes. My advice would therefore be not to rush out and get walking shoes until your baby is walking well by himself, without support. Besides improving his walk and strengthening his feet, this will also save you some money. If you are worried about warmth, dress him in some light socks — though I warn you that he may find it fun to remove them.

## SAFETY TIPS

**Accident-proof your house.** If you have not yet done so, this is the time to do all you can to *prevent* accidents, since your baby is starting to move around. One good example of an important accident-preventing technique is to use plastic covers on electric outlets. These are available at your local hardware store.

**Toys.** All your baby's toys should be unbreakable, too large to swallow, and should never have points or sharp edges.

**Walker.** If your baby uses a walker, make certain that everything that is breakable or potentially dangerous to him is put away. The use of a walker allows your baby to move great distances very rapidly, so you must be on the alert for accidents.

**Burns.** It is a good idea to put guards in front of open heaters and fireplaces, and around radiators. I would strongly advise that you use only flame-retardant sleepwear for your baby; read labels and ask questions of store personnel before buying.

**Kitchen.** The kitchen should be considered a high-risk room. Always remember to keep poisons such as bleach and cleaning agents locked away or on a high shelf. Stop using tablecloths. One of the worst burns I have ever had to treat was that of an eight-month-old who was crawling along the floor, reached up, and yanked at the tablecloth. Unfortunately, there was a large pot of freshly brewed coffee on the table at the time. The entire contents of the pot spilled over the baby's face, chest, and abdomen. The result of all this was a two-month hospitalization for severe second degree burns from which the baby thankfully recovered — but the child is now left with permanent scarring.

**Drowning.** NEVER LEAVE YOUR BABY ALONE IN THE BATH FOR ANY REASON. It takes only a few seconds for an infant to drown, and the water level of the bath does not have to more than a few inches for this tragedy to occur.

## EMOTIONAL (SOCIAL) DEVELOPMENT

Your little baby is now full of curiosity while becoming more and more aware of his surroundings. He will start to show signs of humor, demand attention, distinguish different tones of voice, and learn to recognize himself in a mirror. His attention span is lengthening and he is becoming more selective in his activities. He continues to enjoy audience response to his exploits and he never seems to tire of performing for his close friends. He also will develop fear of being separated from his mother and still remains frightened of strangers.

The question of whether or not the mother should go back to work often comes up around this time. The entire subject of the working mother will be discussed in the chapter on twelve- to eighteen-month olds. If you must go back to work or prefer to go back to work, I would suggest that you read what I have to say about the subject in Chapter V. My observations about working mothers are the same for the six- to nine-month period as they are for the nine- to twelve-month period and beyond.

### SPECIFIC RECOMMENDATIONS

The specific recommendations that follow will help your baby achieve the very best in emotional stability and maturity during this time. They are in large measure the same recommendations I put forth in the two previous chapters, but they are equally important now. The appropriate games and toys will be covered in the section on mental development, but it is clear that many of the activities specifically geared to help your baby develop intellectually will also help his emotional and social development.

**Tone of voice.** As I have already stated, this is more important than you may think. Keep your screaming and yelling to a minimum. The axiom you must never forget is that children learn mainly by example. Although your baby may not yet understand the actual meaning of the words you use, he certainly knows the difference between angry words and happy words. It is not easy to maintain a cheerful and loving disposition twenty-four hours a day, especially when you are overworked and tired from lack of sleep, as parents of young children often are. Nevertheless, you should do your best to be as relaxed and calm as possible while you are with your baby.

**Sounds.** Babies at this age are very interested in all sorts of sounds, and so it is a good idea to have a radio or a record playing as often and for as long as possible. Human voices and music are pleasurable for the baby and give him a sense of well-being and security, especially when you are not around.

**Quality time.** When you are with your baby, try to give him your undivided attention. I can guess what you are thinking. How in the world can I get all my work done if I have to spend so much time playing with my baby? Obviously, there are limits to what you can be expected to do, especially if there are other children in your family. However, you should think about priorities. For example, what is more important, a vacuumed rug or a happy baby? The interesting thing about all this is that if you spend ''quality'' time with your baby, you will build up enough trust and self-esteem in him so that he will be less demanding and clinging. A baby who is encouraged to develop a positive self-image by parents who spend quality time playing and interacting with him is more likely to be happy by himself with his thoughts and toys. During these times you can get the vacuuming done.

**Mood changes.** Rapid mood changes occur very frequently during this time. Be prepared for them and do not worry about them. The most emotionally stable baby is likely to show these dramatic changes in disposition; they are not signs of emotional deprivation.

**Stranger anxiety.** The fear of strangers is quite common throughout most of these three months. Your baby is becoming more selective and discriminating and is no longer attracted to each and every person he

sees. It would be a mistake to force him to stay with a so-called "stranger" (even if the stranger is your favorite uncle) if he is unhappy and frightened about it.

***Privacy.*** All of us need some time for ourselves, and your little baby is no exception. If he is playing quietly and happily, practicing his many motor and beginning verbal skills, he should not be distracted. For example, if he wakes up from a nap in a good mood, is babbling away and playing with his toys, leave him alone. He will let you know soon enough when he becomes tired of being by himself.

***Spanking and/or yelling.*** It is an utter waste of your time to try to force your baby to obey you at this age. He can't understand what you have in mind, and so spanking or yelling are not only ineffective, they frighten him as well. If he enjoys smashing dishes, for example (which was a favorite pastime of my son at this age), simply remove them from his vicinity and give him something unbreakable to drop instead.

***Feelings.*** Your baby is a little person with feelings that are no different from yours or mine. We all seem to forget this from time to time. Keeping this in mind will make it much easier for you to respond to his needs and will also make it easier for you to get through some of his "bad" days. All of us have days when, as the old saying goes, "It just doesn't pay to get out of bed." The very same thing holds true for your little baby.

***Reading aloud.*** I believe that this is a good time to start reading to your child at bedtime. This ritual should be continued for as long as possible. At this age he will not understand the words or even the simplest story you read, but it will be very useful in promoting closeness, warmth, and comfort before he goes off to sleep.

A final thought before we leave this section. What really counts most is for you to *like* being with your baby and for your baby to *like* being with you. If you feel happy together, there really is no way you can go wrong.

## MENTAL (INTELLECTUAL) DEVELOPMENT

Between six and nine months of age your baby will make tremendous advances in his intellectual capacities. With a little help from you he will sharpen his mental skills in order to satisfy his continuing thirst for knowledge. He will begin to learn the consequences of his behavior, and start to imitate and even to understand the meaning of a few words. His memory will get better each day and he will begin to learn to solve simple problems.

## SPECIFIC SUGGESTIONS

The following are specific suggestions which I believe will assist him in achieving his full mental development during these three very interesting months of his life.

**Imitation.** This can be divided into two separate parts. In the first, imitate his sounds, such as his clapping, banging on a table, or even throwing things. Take the lead from your baby. As he does something, simply imitate his action. This will teach him what imitation is all about.

The next step is for you to make simple sounds to him, such as da, pa, ma, clicking your tongue, or coughing, asking him to imitate you. If he learns to respond, it is the real beginning of word vocalization.

The second part of imitation involves games. Examples would be waving bye-bye, clapping your hands, and an old-time favorite, pat-a-cake. For those of you who may be unfamiliar with this seventeenth-century rhyme, it goes as follows:

*Pat-a-cake*
*Pat-a-cake*
*Baker's man*
*Bake me a cake*
*As fast as you can*
*Roll it and pat it*
*And mark it with a B*
*And put it in the oven*
*For baby and me.*

I must admit that before researching this book, I only knew the first five lines, and so my two children were taught a shortened version by their pediatrician-father.

**Cause-and-effect exercises.** It is easy to make up your own exercises. They are extremely useful in helping your baby learn this basic intellectual tool. When and if he is successful, he will respond with a great sense of accomplishment. The key to all learning is repetition. It would be unrealistic for you to expect your baby at this age to learn a cause-and-effect concept without a great deal of repetition. Some simple examples of cause-and-effect games are turning the light on and off and turning a water faucet on and off. First you do it and then you let him try, over and over again. Don't be disappointed if it takes awhile for him to do it successfully. Yet another example of a cause-and-effect game would be to attach a string to an object or toy, show your baby how to pull the string in order to pull the object or toy to you, and then let him have a try. When he learns to do it correctly, respond appropriately and show him how happy and proud you are.

*Talking.* The idea is to talk to your baby and at the same time show him with gestures what you mean. For example, hold your arms out and say, "come," as you reach to pick him up. Say, "bye-bye," and wave your arm at the same time. When you say, "no-no," to him, shake your finger. This is the time to start to teach your baby the meaning of words. If, for example, he is eating hot food, tell him that it's hot. If he touches hot water, tell him that it is hot. If you do this often enough, he will learn to understand the meaning of the word and he will not forget it. If you are consistent and do not try to teach him too many meanings too rapidly, he will make steady progress. As I have already pointed out, many mothers and fathers make the mistake — unknowingly, of course — of not talking much to their baby until he starts talking himself, which usually begins at around one and a half to two years of age. Six- to nine-month-old babies can learn the meaning of some words without being able to say them. It has been my experience and the experience of others that first-borns usually speak earlier than subsequent siblings. The reason for this is that a parent usually spends more time talking to the first baby simply because there is more time to do so. With the birth of the next child the work load increases. Now there is less time to talk to the newest baby since his older brother or sister demands more and more of your attention.

*Mirror.* A mirror is an effective method of teaching your baby to recognize himself. Put him on your lap facing a mirror and say, "Look, there's Billy" (unless your baby's name happens to be Robert).

*Problem solving.* This is extremely important in stretching your baby's mental capacities. Figure out ways of giving him something to think about by creating simple problems. For example, place an object in his

way as he crawls along. Instead of always handing him his rattle, sometimes hide it behind you or off to one side and shake it to get his attention. He will then learn to localize the sound of the rattle and will take off
after it. When he finds it he will be overjoyed, and you should be too.

*Play objects.* The more, the better. Always make sure that the objects
you supply are not small enough for your baby to swallow. Some favorites are balls, stacking toys, plastic cups, soft blocks, and squeaky toys.

## GAMES

*Rhythm games.* These are lots of fun, besides being an important tool
for learning. I am referring to such masterpieces of poetry as This little
piggy went to market; One, two, buckle my shoe; and Hickory, dickory
dock. These and many others are available on records. Another good
idea is to play music and dance and sway to the rhythm, or, if you
prefer, clap your hands in time to the rhythm of the music.

*Dropping games.* These can be a problem for parents who have a bad
back. Your baby will learn to pick up, hold, let go of, and drop an
object, and he becomes an expert in short order. He also never tires of
this activity. One sensible suggestion would be to keep handy a bag full
of objects to be dropped such as spoons and cups. Hand the baby one
object at a time from the bag rather than using the same object each
time. This way you do not have to bend down continually to pick up
what he dropped.

*Floor games.* Too few parents get down on the floor with their babies.
The floor is a fine place to get to know each other. One floor game that
your baby certainly will enjoy and learn from is to put one of his familiar
toys on a piece of cloth that he can grab and pull. Put the toy and cloth
out of his reach and let him crawl to them. Show him how to pull the
cloth so that it will bring the toy closer to him. This is an important
concept, and one that he can easily learn and remember.

*Hide-and-seek games.* You can easily improvise any number of these
games. Peek-a-boo is a favorite. Another is to cover your baby's favorite
toy with a cloth or blanket and say to him, "Find the toy." If nothing
happens—and it probably won't—show him the toy under the cloth or
blanket and then repeat the whole process. A third idea would be to put
one of his balls in a box and close the cover and say, "Find the ball."
This activity will teach him how to open the box and then reach in for

61

the ball. I remember getting a call from the father of an eight-month-old boy. He was terribly upset because little Michael could not learn to open the lid of his toy box. I was even more upset than Mr. B. when he told me that he raised his voice and became angry with his little boy because of this. Never frustrate or tease or get angry with your baby if he fails to accomplish a given task. He feels bad enough about not being successful since he is trying his best. He must be encouraged rather than put down for his efforts.

**Building and stacking games.** Different-size jars or cups that fit easily inside one another are useful for these games, as are various building blocks. Again, it is important to show your baby how to build and how to stack and at the same time tell him in words what you are doing.

This might be a good time to reemphasize that the various recommendations I have outlined are not carved in stone. In other words, there is no reason to follow each and every one. Choose the games and activities you and your baby enjoy doing together. The crucial point is that positive parenting requires quality time spent with the baby. This time can be spent in your lap, in your arms, next to him in his infant seat, or on the floor together. The actual number of minutes or hours you spend is not nearly as important as the way you spend the time. That brain inside your little baby's head is ready, willing, and able to absorb, learn, and develop. It is up to you to furnish the necessary stimuli, tools, and encouragement.

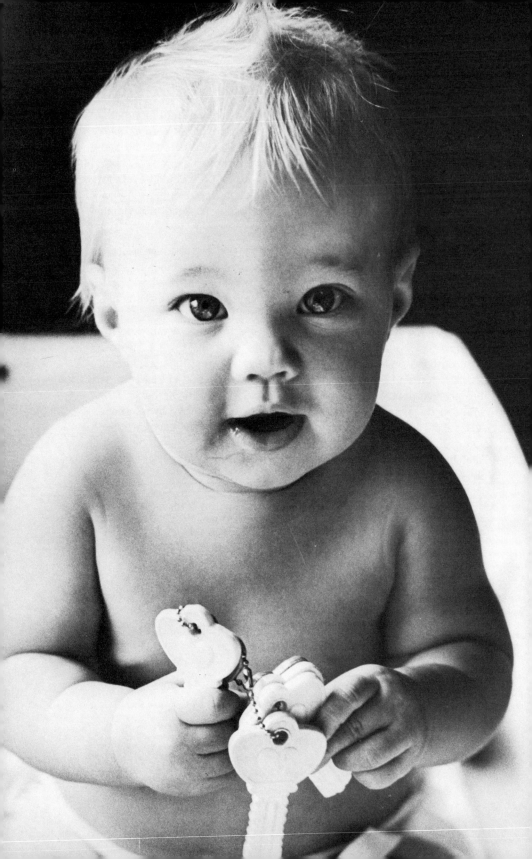

# CHAPTER IV

# Nine to
# Twelve Months

## INTRODUCTION

These three months are an exciting time for your baby and a tiring time for you. The early exploratory phase (six to nine months) has passed, and now the real fun begins. I call this the Four C's Phase:

1. Curiosity
2. Crawling
3. Climbing
4. Cruising

The result of all this activity leads to a very fatigued mother more often than not. In addition, this period can easily become a time of stress and anxiety for all concerned. If your baby is not watched every single minute as she happily cruises and climbs all over the house, a serious accident may occur. I will never forget what a mother of a frisky ten-and-a-half-month-old girl once told me: "Would you believe that I found Barbara sitting on top of the stove with a big grin on her face. She got there by climbing up on a chair. I just never realized that she was so agile and could climb so skillfully." Luckily, dinner was not not being prepared at that time. After a full day of watching and chasing after an active baby, it isn't surprising that a mother becomes exhausted, tense, and upset.

Your baby's remarkable advances in motor skills now include being able to focus on the world of objects around her and the improving ability to transfer these objects from one hand to another, as well as the highly developed skill of being able to pick up even the smallest item (pincer movement of the fingers). In addition, she is beginning to learn about the characteristics of objects: their shape, size, and what they can do. Can it roll or not, is it heavy or light, smooth or rough, hot or cold? And, of course, everything she gets her hands on automatically goes right into her mouth.

A number of studies have shown that groups of children who do poorly academically in elementary school did not test out poorly (in intelligence, motor ability, language, and social development) at one year of age. It is not until two to three years of age that these deficits begin to be noted after testing. Despite this, most authorities on infant and early childhood development agree that these poor achievers are started on that road because they lacked proper stimulation during the first year of life. I am convinced that this nine- to twelve-month period of a baby's life is crucial in terms of her future achievement, both educationally and emotionally. Based on my experience and the experience of many others, it is clear that the extra effort you put in before your baby reaches her first birthday is very important for her subsequent intellectual and social development. Let me add that these three months are also crucial to her future physical well-being. I will discuss this in detail in the section on physical development.

Another major advance seen during these three months is the real beginning of *language* learning. Some babies may actually say their first meaningful words, and this is a time for celebration. On the other hand, there is really no reason to worry if your baby has not said a single recognizable word by the time she is eating a piece of her first birthday cake.

**Myth:** *The earlier a baby talks, the smarter she is.* Or: late talking is a sign of less-than-average intelligence. Not true. There is absolutely no correlation between the age at which a baby starts to talk and her future intellectual capacity. A good example of this is my brother. Among other things, he has been a professor of electrical engineering at M.I.T. and a computer specialist who, according to our mother, did not say his first meaningful word until just before age two. Of much greater significance is that your baby *understand* the meaning of words and sentences and the association of words with their properties (see the growth and development charts). Between nine to twelve months of age, most babies who may or may not say any words understand quite a bit of what they hear you say.

You will notice that your baby is now beginning to realize that older people can be called upon for help. Although babies at this stage cannot yet verbalize their wants, they are able to ask for assistance by gesturing, babbling, pointing, and shouting. Those parents who are attuned and interested can easily recognize what their baby wants most of the time.

A unique aspect of this period is the long periods of time your baby spends just staring at various objects. I recall a mother asking me about her eleven-month-old, who simply stared for minutes on end at the stove, "What do you think she is thinking about?" Obviously I could not answer her but I was pleased that she realized that her baby could, in fact, think. It is important always to remember that babies can think.

Most babies at this age continue to be basically quite friendly and cheerful. They love to be hugged and held and to be kissed, and some learn to kiss you back. You should be prepared, however, for the beginning of negative behavior. Many nine- to twelve-month-olds now become stubborn and less cooperative. These traits frequently show up when they are taking a bath or when food is put on their plates. It is foolish to take this behavior personally. Your baby is not purposely trying to upset and antagonize you. This negative streak is to be expected and should be considered perfectly normal behavior at this age.

Along with the onset of negative behavior comes teething. Teething can cause many babies a good deal of pain and discomfort, so besides being uncooperative and pig-headed, your baby may also be cranky and uncomfortable. The usual sequence for the deciduous or baby teeth to erupt is as follows: The two lower central incisors (bottom center of mouth) come in at around six to seven months of age, and the four upper central incisors appear somewhere between seven and twelve months of age. Occasionally, this sequence is not followed, and this is no reason to be upset. I guarantee that your baby will end up with her full complement of twenty baby teeth sooner or later.

**Myth:** *A delay in teething is related to retarded development.* This is ridiculous. There is no correlation between the age the teeth break through and future development or intelligence. A twelve-month-old with bare gums has just as good a chance of winning the Nobel Prize as a one-year-old with six teeth already in place.

Before moving on to the growth and development charts, let me again remind you that the primary caretaker, whether mother, father, or somebody else, remains the key to your baby's positive development. Your baby learns most from the person who spends most of the time with her. She watches the primary caretaker for approval, to see what she can or cannot do, and for language learning. But it is also true that she can relate to and learn from more than just one primary caretaker. Aside from any surrogate who takes care of the baby for whatever reason, both mother and father ideally should function as coprimary caretakers. In my experience, a baby who is blessed with both a mother and father who practice quality parenting has the best chance to achieve her maximum potential, emotionally, intellectually, and physically. By the time the candles are lit for her first birthday party, she will be well on her way along the right road.

## 9 – 12 Months

### GROWTH AND DEVELOPMENT
*Physical (Motor)*

#### 9 – 10 Months

1. Stands with little or no support.
2. Walks a few steps holding on.
3. Climbs up and down from a low chair.
4. Can now sit down from a standing position.
5. Can carry two objects in one hand.
6. Adept at transferring objects from one hand to another.
7. Skillful use of "pincer" movement.
8. Cruises along furniture.

#### 10 – 11 Months

1. Stands alone.
2. Begins to be able to climb stairs.

3. Walks with only a little support, holding one hand.
4. Begins to be able to pull socks off.
5. Able to use a spoon to feed herself and to splatter the walls.
6. Can hold a crayon or a pencil and scribble with them.
7. Picks up tiny objects.

### 11 – 12 Months

1. Walks alone, a few steps.
2. Climbs up and down stairs.
3. Also may climb out of playpen or crib.
4. Helps undress herself.
5. Handles crayon and pencil more skillfully.
6. Still prefers crawling rapidly around the house.
7. Goes from standing to sitting easily and speedily.

*Note:* These charts are based on average *ranges* of growth and development; many normal babies perform and achieve either sooner or later than indicated.

### 9 – 12 Months

## GROWTH AND DEVELOPMENT
### Emotional (Social)

### 9 – 10 Months

1. Imitates various facial expressions and different sounds.
2. Shows signs of jealousy, especially of other children.
3. Well attuned to approval and disapproval from her audience.
4. Looking for fun and attention; e.g., taking hat off and putting it back on, over and over again.
5. Becoming protective of her various possessions.
6. Rapid mood changes, from happy to sad to hurt to angry to cranky.
7. Afraid of unfamiliar places.

### 10 – 11 Months

1. Enjoys music and rhythmic sounds.
2. Becomes very dependent on her mother or primary caretaker.
3. Less cooperative and more stubborn.
4. Understands meaning of "no."
5. Learns to tease parents to gain attention.

6. Continually seeking approval.
7. Enjoys being hugged and cuddled, and hugs back.
8. Expresses many emotions and understands them in others.

### 11 — 12 Months

1. Good understanding of self, has learned that she's a separate and distinct person.
2. Upset when separated from mother or primary caretaker.
3. Fears strangers and new places.
4. Negative behavior, including temper tantrums and being uncooperative, especially with eating.
5. Emotionally labile: switches moods rapidly and often without any apparent reason.
6. Recognizes various and different emotions in the people around her.
7. Developing excellent sense of humor.
8. Becoming more selective in activities and in who she relates to.

*Note:* These charts are based on avergae *ranges* of growth and development; many normal babies perform and achieve either sooner or later than indicated.

## 9 — 12 Months

### GROWTH AND DEVELOPMENT
*Mental (Intellectual)*

### 9 — 10 Months

1. May say a word or two such as "mama" or "dada" and understand it.
2. Starts to carry out simple commands such as "Give me the ball."
3. May reach for an object without actually seeing it; e.g., for a doll that is behind her.
4. Begins to understand the concept of space; e.g., realizes that an object that is moved can be moved back.
5. Starts to differentiate the various properties of objects; e.g., throws a ball, shakes a rattle, builds blocks, crumples paper.
6. Starts associating words with gestures; e.g., say "bye-bye" and baby waves.

### 10 — 11 Months

1. Begins to understand the meanings of many words. May say a couple of simple words.

2. Efficient at imitating gestures and expressions of others.
3. May be able to point to various parts of her body.
4. Starts to associate meaning of words and their properties; e.g., bird and the sky, or a dog and barking.
5. Can place small objects into a container and also can remove them.
6. Can look for hidden objects.
7. Looks at pictures in a book and begins to be able to turn pages, usually a few at a time.
8. Can pull off socks and untie shoelaces.

## 11 – 12 Months

1. May be able to say a few words and understand their meaning.
2. Babbles short, unintelligible sentences.
3. Memory improving; remembers past experiences for longer periods of time.
4. Becomes involved in problem-solving by trial and error.
5. Can build a tower of 2 or 3 blocks.
6. Increased understanding of the association of words with their properties; e.g., say "airplane," and she looks up at the sky.
7. Understands meaning of more and more words and short sentences.
8. Starts to be able to group objects by class; e.g., by size or shape or color.
9. Can carry out a number of different simple commands.
10. Learns to find hidden objects.

Note: These charts are based on average *ranges* of growth and development; many normal babies perform and achieve either sooner or later than indicated.


## PHYSICAL (MOTOR) DEVELOPMENT

### NUTRITION

A baby who has been breast fed up until now certainly can be continued on breast milk until she reaches one year of age or even older. If during this period you decide to stop breast feeding, I would suggest that you switch over to one of the commercially prepared formulas. This is in keeping with the current recommendation of the Committee on Nutrition of the American Academy of Pediatrics. Their recommendation is to use formula rather than regular cow's milk until the baby has reached one year of age. Many breast-feeding mothers who switch during this three-month period put their infants on regular whole milk instead of formula, and I have no serious objection to this. By nine months of age a normal infant can handle the extra salt and protein in regular milk without any difficulty.

If you have been feeding your baby formula for the first nine months, my recommendation is to continue this type of feeding up until one year of age. However, if the decision is made to switch to regular cow's milk instead of formula, this is also acceptable.

What about solid foods?

Babies at this age should be introduced to a variety of nutritious foods one by one. You should always wait a few days after starting the baby on a new food to make certain that she can tolerate it. Your baby should now be offered three well-balanced meals each day. Many babies are introduced to regular table foods during this period, while still others prefer strained or junior foods. As I stated earlier, you should not add salt and sugar. Your child's food preferences and eating patterns are being established, and this should always be uppermost in your mind as you prepare her meals. A nutritious food that you should introduce at this time, if you have not already done so between six and nine months, is yogurt, preferably of the plain variety. Many adults find plain yogurt very tart-tasting and prefer it with added fruits, but your baby may well enjoy it just as it is. There is no reason to assume automatically that your baby requires the yogurt to be sweetened.

There is one aspect of nutrition that upsets many parents at this time, and that is the fact that many babies suddenly rebel against food. The battle lines are drawn. The mother does everything in her power to force the food down the baby's throat. The baby in turn does everything in her power to refuse to eat, spitting the food out and/or pushing it away. Through the years I have received innumerable frantic phone calls from distraught mothers complaining bitterly to me about this problem. My stock answer is that I have yet to see a baby starve when food is available. A favorite story from my collection concerns a phone call from the mother of an eleven-month-old boy. She was extremely upset because Joseph stopped drinking his juice. "Dr. Eden, what should I do? If this goes on much longer, I am sure he will get scurvy." What I told that mother, and what I am now telling you, is not to worry as long as multivitamins are given to your baby.

The important point to remember is that it is normal and usual for many nine- to twelve-month-olds to show a marked decrease in their appetites. The reason simply is that growth slows down and less food is required at this time. If you understand and expect this to happen, you should be able to stop worrying about it.

At this age, a number of babies can hold and manipulate a cup and a spoon. Some babies like to feed themselves, even as much as a whole meal. Others like to feed themselves only so-called "finger foods" such as crackers, pieces of banana, and cheese. Still others prefer to sit back and have you do all the work. By one year of age many babies are pretty adept at spoon-feeding themselves. I would encourage you to allow your baby to feed herself even though she may make a mess of the entire feeding area.

What is really most important is to allow your baby to eat as much or as little as she wants rather than as much as you think she needs. Mealtimes for the nine- to twelve-month-old should be relaxed and cheerful, free of tension and stress. As a matter of fact, this concept holds true for any age. Unfortunately, this often is not the case during these three months. Within reason, leave the choice of foods to your baby. If a well-balanced meal is placed on her plate, the chances are good that she will choose just what her body needs over the long run. This is not simply wishful thinking on my part. A famous experiment was carried out by Dr. Clara Davis on a group of one-year-olds who were allowed to choose freely from a variety of nutritious foods. During the course of the study there was absolutely no adult involvement in the feeding. The results were astonishing. The babies ended up eating a perfectly well-balanced diet over the period of the experiment.

What do I mean by a well-balanced diet? This is a diet that contains daily servings from each of the four basic food groups.

1. Meat: includes meat, poultry, and fish, with alternatives of eggs, dried beans, and soy beans.
2. Vegetable and fruit: includes all fruits and vegetables.
3. Milk: includes milk, cheese, yogurt, and various milk products.
4. Breads and cereals: includes breads and cereals that are whole-grained, enriched, or restored; also includes rice and pasta.

It makes no difference at which meal these foods are given. The important point to remember is that your baby should be offered a variety of nutritious foods from all of these four basic food groups each day.

I will get into the subject of between-meal snacks and so-called "junk foods" in greater detail in a later chapter. As far as your nine- to twelve-month-old is concerned, let me point out that you should not fall into the trap of giving your baby snacks when she is cranky or bored. This will start a bad habit that will be difficult to break later on. Just think about how many of us, as adolescents and adults, go on eating binges when we feel sorry for ourselves or are frustrated. The axiom to keep in mind is that food should never be substituted for love. Instead of feeding your baby when she is irritable and cranky, give her a kiss or play a game with her instead.

Iron-deficiency anemia is most commonly seen in the one- to two-year-old age group. If this anemia is of sufficient severity, it may lead to serious problems. Included among the possible consequences of severe protracted iron-deficiency anemia are increased irritability and fatigue, growth retardation, and decreased resistance to infection. Of great significance is the possible association of iron-deficiency anemia and altered behavior. Studies in older children have shown a relationship between severe anemia and lower I.Q.s, decreased attention spans, and perceptual difficulties. One recent study involving infants nine to twenty-six months of age demonstrated increased scores on a Mental Development Index after their anemias were treated. The nine- to twelve-month-old period is notorious for the start of iron-deficiency anemia. Babies at this age are often switched to cow's milk. At the same time there is a decrease in their appetites. The result is that many of these babies eat very little solid food and drink a great deal of regular milk. This type of diet is very low in iron. These are the babies who, when tested between one and two years of age, are found to have profound iron-deficiency conditions. I am calling all this to your attention now so you will be in a position to *prevent* it from happening. It is essential that you continue your baby on infant cereals (iron fortified) as well as offering her the well-balanced diet I have outlined. If your baby is drinking cow's milk, make certain that she doesn't drink over one quart per day so that she will have enough appetite left to eat iron-containing solid foods. If your baby looks pale, or if, despite your best efforts, she only drinks milk, your doctor should be consulted. A simple finger-prick blood test can determine if your baby is anemic. If she is, she will be given supplemental iron. Treatment is very effective and the anemia can be corrected within a short period of time. These simple suggestions will guarantee that your baby will never develop severe iron-deficiency with its possible adverse effects on learning in school later on.

## EXERCISE

There is no problem at all with the great majority of nine- to twelve-month-olds when it comes to physical exercise. Rather, the more usual

problem is trying to slow them down. With all their crawling, cruising, walking, and climbing triggered off by their great continuing curiosity, these little babies tone up and develop their muscles and coordination from morning until night. All your baby needs is the space and opportunity, and her adventurous spirit will do the rest. As I have already told you, one of the consequences of this great amount of physical activity is an increased risk of accidents, and the prevention of accidents at this age will be covered in the section on safety tips later on in this chapter.

You should be aware of a group of babies who do not follow this usual pattern of physical activity. These nine- to twelve-month-olds are more placid and less active and are content to sit around a good deal of the time, drinking excessive amounts of milk and munching on cookies and the like. It is true that some of this behavior pattern probably is genetically determined, but I believe that most of it is due to improper parenting. A good number of these basically sedentary babies are already fat, having been overfed and overstuffed from day one. The vicious cycle has been started. It really does not matter which came first, the obesity or the inactivity. The fatter the baby, the more inactive she becomes. And so if your baby is obese — and you don't have to weigh her to know it; just look at her and it will be obvious — do something about it right now. Cut down on the total quantity of milk and fattening foods (usually the so-called "junk foods") such as sugary cookies and make greater efforts to get her moving out of her infant seat or crib. Offer her a piece of apple rather than a chocolate-chip cookie.

Another factor which leads to a placid, inactive baby is overprotection and overconcern with her physical well-being. In my experience, mothers more often than fathers are guilty of this. They lose sight of the long-term damage they are inflicting on the physical as well as emotional development of the baby. By continually discouraging physical activity because of their fear of an accident, they inadvertently destroy the natural curiosity that is so crucial to the healthy development of the baby. I recently made a house call to see a one-year-old girl who had a fever and a severe respiratory infection. As I walked in I was immediately struck by the immaculately clean house, with no clutter or mess, no toys on the floor, and everything neatly in place. After examining Christina and advising Mrs. S. about treatment of the illness, I asked her if her house was always so neat. "Absolutely; I pride myself on keeping a clean and tidy house," she answered. From my point of view I would have been happier to see a messy, cluttered, lived-in house, which is to be expected with a baby around. Incidentally, Christina was markedly overweight and inactive, and I understood the reason why.

My advice is not to curtail your baby's desire to explore and roam. Accidents can be prevented by removing those objects that might be dangerous to the baby as well as those objects that she can easily destroy. For some unexplained, mysterious reason, a large number of babies at this age are fascinated by stairways. During this period, if given the chance, some of them learn to navigate the stairs, both up and down. This is certainly a good exercise, but if not carefully supervised, can also be quite dangerous. A simple gate blocking the stairway when you are not around or are unavailable to participate in this splendid activity is the solution.

I would suggest that you should take your baby outdoors as often as you can. She will welcome the change and will also have more opportunities to exercise her sturdy legs and body. Many nine- to twelve-month-olds walk with a little support, and such an activity is to be encouraged. Less carrying around, fewer trips in the carriage or stroller, and more walking pay off later on in helping her become more active and agile. Discouraging babies from moving around enough now helps lead to an inactive and sedentary life style later on.

I would like to again remind you that babies are sturdy and strong, and they love to be handled and to participate in roughhouse activities. Besides being a great source of pleasure, wrestling and tumbling around develops and strengthens all their muscles. These little girls and boys are not nearly as fragile as you might be led to believe, and they need not be handled with extreme care and caution. Obviously, sensible limits should be set in order to avoid an accident.

There are some games and materials that will help your baby's physical development during this period. From the following list you will see that it is not necessary to buy any special exercise equipment or apparatus.

**"Go get it" games.** These will be discussed in detail in the mental development section.

**Hide-and-seek games.** These are all good exercise and give a baby practice in moving around, whether it's crawling or cruising and occasionally walking. Many variations can be tried. For example, finger dexterity can be developed by wrapping a toy in a piece of paper and then showing your baby how to get the toy out. As the baby tires of one hide-and-seek game, try another.

**Pots and pans (and various sturdily constructed toys).** One of the activities fascinating to most babies between nine and twelve months is

banging, and although this can be pretty noisy, it is fine exercise besides being a most satisfying pastime. Elizabeth was eleven months old and her mother told me about her loud, rhythmic banging together of two favorite pots for long, nonstop sessions. "You know, Dr. Eden, she practices every single day. There is no question in my mind that I'm raising the first great female drummer."

**Balls.** Various-sized balls, all large enough not to be swallowed or to cause choking, are great fun and a ready source of exercise. Footballs are a favorite since they bounce in all sorts of directions. Besides chasing the ball, your baby starts to learn to throw the ball and even sometimes to catch it. This is important for her future since instilling skills in sports is an integral part of achieving maximum physical well-being throughout life. This concept will be discussed at greater length in subsequent chapters.

## SAFETY TIPS

Parents must now really be on the alert to prevent accidents. Statistics show that more and more accidents occur as the baby navigates around the house, crawling, cruising, and climbing.

**Poisons and drugs.** These must always be kept not only out of reach but out of sight. Aspirin, liquor, cigarettes, furniture polish, laundry detergents, and the like all can seriously hurt or even kill your baby. If you remember that babies at this age are naturally curious and adventuresome and that everything they grab goes directly into their mouths, you will act accordingly. It is good practice to always use child-safe packaging for all medicines. I recommend that you have some syrup of ipecac readily available at all times. This is an emetic (a drug that induces vomiting) and can be used if your baby does swallow a poison or drug. Always check with your doctor first because ipecac should not be given automatically for all possible poisoning cases. For example, vomiting should not be induced when your child swallows a petroleum or lye product. You might also want to have a first-aid booklet on hand for such emergencies.

**Automobile travel.** When traveling by car, always use one of the child-restraint systems that are on the market. Not only will they reduce the possibility and number of serious automobile injuries, but this practice will get both you and your child accustomed to the use of restraints. Studies have proven that this early introduction to safety restraints in automobiles is the only way to assure that as she grows up she will continue to use them. This safety tip is obviously important for her future physical well-being. Finally, set a proper example for your baby by using an appropriate seat belt or harness yourself every time you use your car.

**Falls.** There is no way to avoid falls, but you can help prevent serious injuries from falls by taking some simple safety measures. Place gates across stairways and lower the crib mattress as your baby starts to stand and climb. I remember two serious falls that occurred the same day. One happened to a ten-month-old boy who climbed out of his crib and landed on his head with a resultant concussion. In the other, an eleven-month-old girl fell down half a flight of stairs. Luckily, both of these babies were not seriously hurt, but your child may not be as fortunate.

**Dangerous objects.** Since your baby is now always on the move, exploring and learning, it is necessary to keep a step ahead of her. Objects such as knives, scissors, razors, and breakables must be put away. Play areas must be cleared of sharp-edged furniture. This advice may seem too obvious to you. Maybe so, but I have treated too many accidents involving such objects to take anything for granted.

**Bathrooms.** Babies love to play with and in water at this age — in the toilet, bathtub, or sink. *Never* leave your baby alone near wtaer, even for a second. It doesn't take very long to drown.

**Smoking.** Although I have cautioned you earlier on smoking, I want to emphasize the dangers by repeating my warnings here. Be careful with lighted cigarettes; they can very easily start a fire. Better yet, try to stop smoking altogether. You might be motivated to give this a try if you are aware of a number of studies that have proven that there are more frequent hospitalizations and doctor visits during the first year for babies living in houses where the adults smoke than among babies living with nonsmoking parents. These serious illnesses are usually respiratory diseases such as pneumonia and bronchitis, and it takes little imagination to figure out why. Cigarette smoke is not only harmful to the smoker but causes extra trouble for the baby breathing in the polluted air.

## EMOTIONAL (SOCIAL) DEVELOPMENT

As I have already stated and will continue to emphasize throughout the book, your goal should be a happy, well-adjusted child. Such a person has a much better chance of becoming a well-adjusted adult. You, the parents, are the key to whether she will grow up emotionally healthy and with an intact sensitivity or emotionally maladjusted and with a blunted sensitivity. All of us want a cheerful, contented baby who will continue that way at age two years and beyond. None of us relish the thought of raising a baby who will turn out to be spoiled, self-centered, nasty, and angry by the age of two and who will probably then stay that way as she grows up. Your approach, input, and attitude *now* will in large measure determine which direction your baby's emotional and social development takes.

Before going on to discuss my specific recommendations, let me remind you of the following normal emotional developmental milestones of the nine- to twelve-month-old (listed in more detail in the growth and development chart earlier in this chapter):

1. Start of negative behavior — less cooperative and more stubborn
2. Temper tantrums
3. Emotional lability (rapid mood changes)
4. Stronger preferences for certain people and certain activities
5. Great dependency on the primary caretaker, and feels upset at separation from same
6. Craving for approval and attention
7. Teasing behavior

### SPECIFIC RECOMMENDATIONS

Keeping with these traits and characteristics in mind, I offer the following guidelines which I believe will give your baby the best chance of turning out emotionally sound now and in the future.

*Trusting approach.* I purposely put this at the top of the list because it is the most important. What I mean by this is to approach your baby in a way that is both trusting and accepting, and in harmony with her emotional needs. If you believe in and accept the concept that your little girl is dependent and immature and that your role as parent is to meet these needs, the rest is easy. It is normal for your baby to turn to you for help and you should be happy if she does. Parents should encourage in every way their baby's abilities to regulate their own actions and discourage (but not punish) their inconsiderate antisocial behavior.

On the other hand, if you perceive your baby as being selfish and demanding by nature (the distrustful approach), it becomes much more difficult to satisfy her emotional needs. It is a sad but true fact that many parents are sure that their babies are devious, cunning, and manipulative, and so "giving in" to their needs will truly lead to "spoiling" the baby. If after you have read this I have been able to convince you that such an attitude on your part will result in conflict, frustration, stress, and emotional injury, my efforts to help you do the best possible job will be off to a fine start.

Mrs. S. made a special appointment to talk to me about one-year-old Janet and her antisocial behavior and temper tantrums. "It seems as if I am spending most of every day punishing Janet for not behaving like a little lady," were the exact words this distraught mother used in starting our discussion. It took me three separate thirty-minute sessions to try to improve this unhealthy, stressful home situation. Nine-to twelve-month-olds are not "little ladies" or "little gentlemen," and to expect them or try to force them to behave or obey is the wrong approach.

**Overindulgence.** It is not difficult to carry your trusting behavior too far because of the fear of frustrating or antagonizing your baby. It is important not to confuse trust and acceptance with overindulgence. I am not for a minute advocating overpermissiveness, chaos, and anarchy. A certain amount of firmness and discipline are necessary and required for the future emotional and social adjustment of your child. If things start getting out of hand, the most effective method of teaching and disciplining your baby is to distract her or, if that does not work, to remove her from the unacceptable situation. There is nothing wrong with a light but meaningful slap across her behind when nothing else works. The rules of acceptable behavior must be defined and explained. It is important to remember always to be as consistent as possible. There is nothing more confusing and emotionally destructive for a little child than inconsistency in your responses to her actions. Mothers and fathers should try to be consistent in dealing with their baby. My favorite illustration of this confusion involved a couple whose eleven-month-old boy was a dynamo. Bobby's greatest pleasure in life was climbing up and down the stairs. Mama was continually frightened for his safety and Papa couldn't have cared less. You can imagine the tension in the house and the problem

Bobby faced as he tried to figure out what was going on. This problem turned out to be an easy one to solve. I simply advised these parents to purchase and install a movable gate across the stairs, and all was well.

**Goals.** Avoid setting unrealistic goals. This is one suggestion that holds true for children of all ages and it is the one I worry about most as I write this book. It is one of the most important keys in helping your baby develop the emotional backbone and positive self-image that will stay with her forever. You do a great disservice to your baby by pushing her too hard and too fast in your frantic efforts to make her a superchild. Coercive teaching, the too early emphasis on reading and learning words, all should be discouraged. You may suspect that you are setting unrealistic goals if your baby does not enjoy the activities you introduce. If she is happy with a particular activity, the chances are good that it is the right activity for her at that time.

**Restrictions.** Within reason, keep restrictions to a minimum. Playpens, seats, and gates all have their place in the overall scheme of things, but they should be used judiciously. Too many restrictive devices of any kind lead to boredom and a waste of the good time that your baby should enjoy. If you find that you are saying "no" and "don't touch" all day long, there is something wrong and you should take stock of the situation. It may well be that you are not giving your baby her fair share of freedom.

**Privacy.** This is a difficult concept for some parents to understand. It has been my experience that mothers and fathers often believe that they should spend as much time as possible interacting and playing with their babies. Within certain limits they are correct. But it is just as important to realize that the baby also needs some time for herself and some time to play with other children without your active involvement. An integral part of the emotional stability of your baby is for her not to become overdependent and overpossessive of you. Your baby should be given opportunities to play with her toys and be with her thoughts without your participation. When she is content and happy with her privacy, you should be happy for her. Take pride in having helped her achieve this significant degree of emotional maturity at such an early age. "Can you believe it, Amy actually prefers playing with her toys to playing with me?" an upset mother reported to me one afternoon during the well-baby visit. I was very pleased to hear her tell me this but I had a hard time explaining why I felt that way.

*Curiosity.* This remains of vital importance and so it will be repeated and reemphasized. Always keep in mind that your baby must be given every opportunity to satisfy her insatiable curiosity. Many studies have shown that babies who are given the freedom to explore turn out not only more emotionally secure but do better in their academic pursuits later on.

*Rewards.* Reward your baby's accomplishments. This is obvious, but the way to do it may not be as obvious. The most effective method of rewarding accomplishment is with a hug and a kiss and with the right words and tone of voice. "I am so proud of you," is what I like to hear and your baby likes to hear. A reminder: rewarding accomplishment with food is to be discouraged. Food should not be equated with love. More about this in later chapters.

*Talk.* The more, the better. Most nine- to twelve-month-old babies have a very limited or no intelligble vocabulary, but they are beginning to understand the meaning of more and more words. Remember, besides what you say, your tone of voice is really what counts.

*Toys and games.* These will be covered in the following section on mental development. The only one I will mention now is a so-called "busy-bath" toy, of which a number of types are on the market. During this age period almost all babies have a strange fascination with water play, and such a toy serves as a continuous source of pleasure and entertainment for them. Anything that makes your baby happy strengthens her emotional and social stability.

## MENTAL (INTELLECTUAL) DEVELOPMENT

As I suggested at the start of this chapter, your baby's future intellectual achievements will depend in large measure on what she learns long before her first day in class at preschool or in elementary school. The foundation for her mental capabilities and accomplishments must be built now, and this requires the proper stimulation and activities that only you, a primary caretaker, can provide.

An important point to keep in mind is that imitation is the main way your baby learns. I can remember when our son was about twelve months old, we found him seriously babbling away on the telephone one morning. Robert was not using a toy phone. After watching his father answer many phone calls each morning during the hour when parents called for advice, he decided that it was time for him to do the same. Your baby is now beginning to understand the meaning of more and more words. A sign of increasing intellectual capacity is her ability to associate the meaning of some words with their properties (see the growth and development chart). She also is discovering that the sounds she makes are a method of communicating with you rather than just the other way around. Memory is improving. She will make advances in problem solving almost entirely by trial and error.

The opportunities for learning are all around her, not only in the house but in the street, park, automobile, and stores. My advice is to take her out every chance you get and talk to her about what you see and what you are doing together. This is not a waste of your time and effort, even though your baby probably still will not understand most of what you are describing. Your talking encourages her to imitate the sounds she hears. Make it a habit to touch whatever you are talking about if at all possible. Point out a tree, a dog, a car. This allows your baby to begin to associate the word or words you use with the objects you are talking about — and that is what real understanding is all about. Your enthusiasm in showing new places and demonstrating new activities will quickly rub off on the baby. All educators and psychologists agree that motivation and enthusiasm are both essential in order to achieve maximum intellectual academic attainment. It all starts with your ability to share the fun and discovery of learning with your baby.

There are times when parents get carried away with their attempts at trying to teach their babies something they consider important. The illustration that comes to mind is that of an art teacher who took her eleven-month-old daughter Abigail to a museum. Standing with her in front of a magnificent Rembrandt painting, Mrs. P. pointed to the painting and described its beauty, color, and design. All Abigail was interested in was crawling over to a nearby water fountain. The lesson to be learned is for you to expose your baby to as many new experiences and activities as possible but in the final analysis always to allow your baby to decide what she is interested in. Don't force her to participate just because you think it's a good idea.

## GAMES

Babies learn primarily through games. New games are needed to challenge their increasing awareness and intelligence. The interest your baby shows and the length of time she spends with each game or activity should indicate to you whether she is enjoying what she is doing. With each success in figuring out a new game or activity her self-esteem expands and grows. I don't believe that any elaborate, expensive toys or games need be purchased at this time. The following are some games that I believe will stimulate your baby's mental processes to the fullest:

*"Go get it."* This is a floor activity and permits your baby to practice her increasing skills in crawling, in walking with support, or cruising. All you need is a ball. Simply roll it away out of her reach and say, "Go get the ball and bring it to Mommy" (or Daddy, as the case may be). If nothing happens, don't be discouraged, but try again. Encourage her with the proper words and with overt signs of affection. In short order, most babies will get the hang of it, and some will even learn to roll the ball back to you.

The "go-get-it" game can be expanded and continued as you go about doing your household chores with your baby following you around. Ask her to bring you certain objects such as a towel or a pan. She will learn the meaning of new words and also the purpose of the object she fetched. For example, if she brought you a towel, you then can wipe the dishes and tell her that the towel is drying the dish. At the next bath tell her that the towel is wiping her hands and face. This approach also teaches your baby about cooperation and being helpful; as she brings the object to you, say thank you and remind her that she has helped you by her action. Of course, these little "helpers" slow you down considerably with their "help," but it's well worth the extra time.

*Filling and emptying.* This type of game serves the dual purpose of increasing your baby's small muscle skills as well as teaching her about the concept of space (see the growth and development chart). The object of the game is to put various objects into a container and then to take them out. Show your baby how to do it, and always talk to her and explain what you are doing at the same time. This demonstration with words needs to be repeated until your baby can carry out the process by herself. Of course, make certain that there are no sharp-edged objects to cut her or tiny objects to swallow. After she learns how and what to do, leave her alone to practice. Many babies spend a good deal of time filling up and emptying containers, becoming more and more skillful at it, all the while babbling to themselves. Your baby may even at times say "no" to herself when she doesn't do it properly.

**Hide and seek.** Besides the exercise, this game teaches your baby problem solving. For example, put one of her small toys inside a box and then hide the box. She now has a two-step problem, first to find the box and then to open it and remove the toy. These little nine- to twelve-month-olds are amazing in their ability to concentrate and to be very tenacious. After you hide an object, a baby won't give up until she finds it. Make certain, therefore, that you don't hide it too well or you may really frustrate and upset her. When she finally does find the hidden object, tell her how happy and proud you are of her achievement.

**Peek-a-boo.** All sorts of variations on this perennial favorite are possible. Cover your eyes and say, "Where did you go? I can't see you." Then cover her eyes and say, "Where did Daddy go? Gloria can't see me." This is a good teaching and learning experience since many babies at this age think that if they can't see you, you in turn can't see them.

**Slot machine.** All you need for this one is a pile of pennies and an empty plastic cup with a top in which you have cut out a slot. This game is excellent for training in hand dexterity and also serves as a stimulus for your baby's interest in the *results* of her activity, such as dropping objects and then picking them up. The one problem with this game is the possibility that your baby will swallow a penny, but this is no catastrophe if she doesn't choke on it. Mrs. S. called me one evening and said her baby started with fifty pennies, and when the game was over there were forty-seven pennies in the container and two pennies on the floor. You guessed it: the missing penny was found in Jenny's bowel movement four days later. However, you probably should remain with the child during this activity.

**Blocks.** Wooden blocks are fine. These blocks serve to help your baby learn the skill of building. Between nine and twelve months of age many babies are able to build up to three-block towers. They have more fun knocking over the tower than building it, and this can serve as a pleasurable activity for many hours on end.

**Shopping.** The modern supermarket with its shopping carts is an ideal situation for pleasurable learning. As you wheel your baby up and down the aisles in the cart, talk to her about the various foods on the shelves and encourage her to help you put them into the cart. Show her the pictures on the various cans as well as the different fruits and vegetables in the bins. For example, "Here's a tomato. It's red and soft." Come to think of it, since babies love to squeeze objects, maybe a tomato is the wrong example. A head of lettuce is a better idea. After you get home, show her what you do with the different foods you bought. Later, as she eats them, remind her about what you did together in the supermarket.

When I have the opportunity of doing supermarket shopping myself, I am very interested in watching mothers with their babies. One type of mother spends all her time saying "no" and denying the baby a chance to participate, and both mother and baby usually are upset and miserable. The other type of mother involves her baby in the experience. The babies who are encouraged to participate are happier and are learning and expanding their knowledge at a much more rapid rate.

I'd like to close this chapter by doing away with another old wives' tale that is unrelated to anything physical, mental, or emotional but is appropriate to this age.

**Myth:** *Giving a baby a haircut before one year of age brings bad luck.* I don't understand where or how this one started, but it surely is utter nonsense.

Happy first birthday!

# CHAPTER V

# Twelve to Eighteen Months

## INTRODUCTION

"Where does he get all that energy?" I am asked this question over and over again by the parents of twelve- to eighteen-month-olds. The parents of these children are amazed by the tremendous activity of their toddlers, on the move literally from morning until night. If you think you were tired before, during the nine- to twelve-month stage, the real fun is only beginning. These little people, besides showing more independence, impulsiveness, and self-assertion, are still just as curious and adventuresome as before. Your twelve- to eighteen-month-old is beginning to make the discovery of "self." It's as if he seems to shout, "I want to do this my way, by myself, and now!" If you combine all these traits with his increased efficiency in walking and climbing, the results are ob-

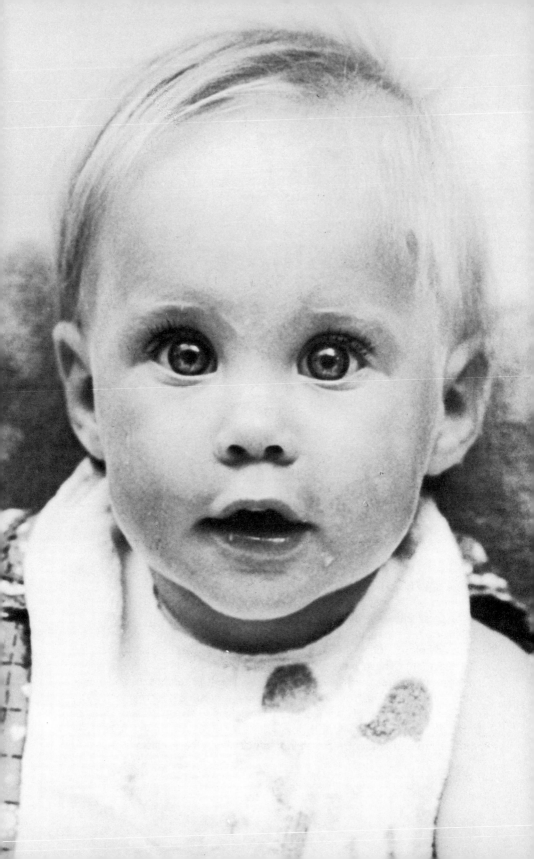

vious. But there is even more to look forward to: the start of negative behavior. The so-called "terrible twos" start earlier than at age two, often some time between fourteen and eighteen months of age. Your youngster now understands the meaning of "no," not only your "no" but his own "no" as well. He becomes stubborn and less cooperative and may refuse to obey your requests or demands. He will also do his best to take over. The result can become a real test of wills. What I am describing is normal behavior for a baby of this age and so it is best that you be prepared to expect it. Do not take it personally, and remember that this too will pass.

Your baby is now able to explore the whole world around him more adequately and efficiently. Since he stands a good deal of the time now, he can see much more than he could before. Now he can see table tops and all the objects on them, bookshelves, television knobs, and all the other fascinating items in his environment. This widening of his horizons is new, interesting, and exciting for him but it creates additional problems for you, especially relating to his safety and the safety of your possessions. At this point you have two basic choices, and the one you make (consciously or unconsciously) will in large measure determine whether you will be successful in achieving the goal of this book; namely, helping your child develop to his maximum potential now and later on in life. You can either basically keep your house for the adults in it or you can "child-proof" it for your baby. If you don't follow any other suggestion I make, please follow this one: "child-proof" your house! (Specific guidelines and recommendations as to how to do so will be listed in the safety section later on in this chapter.) Your toddler needs plenty of room and opportunity to play. Dr. Piaget describes this period as the phase of experimentation. The insatiable curiosity your baby shows must always be encouraged. This approach will surely make him more successful and self-confident later on in school and in his chosen occupation. If his curiosity is squelched at every turn because you are afraid of accidents or the destruction of your possessions, this will certainly lead to a decrease in self-confidence and an increase in self-doubt, and these traits will stay with him throughout his school years and beyond.

All educators agree that success in school is based on the following four factors:

1. Verbal confidence
2. Problem-solving ability
3. Independence, curiosity, and enthusiasm

**4.** Sociability and control of emotions

These six months of your baby's life are critical to achieving all these goals. Each will be covered in detail in the appropriate section of this chapter.

A few words about language are in order at this point. You can expect your baby to say up to six meaningful words by the time he is eighteen months old. He will surely understand many more words and phrases and should be able to respond to simple commands such as, "Give that to me" as you point to a particular object or toy. Since he learns by imitation, it is important that you speak to him slowly and clearly in a calm, quiet tone of voice. When he does say a meaningful word, do not imitate his pronunciation but rather repeat the word to him correctly.

Let me get back to the superenergy of your toddler. His increased activity takes many forms. He loves to throw food, ransack closets, open drawers and throw out everything he can get his little hands on. A mother of a sixteen-month-old described to me in amazement the speed and efficiency with which Andy emptied out an entire drawer full of clothes during the minute or two it took her to go downstairs to answer the doorbell. What was lovely about this mother was that she told me the story with pride and pleasure rather than with frustration and anger. These young explorers climb into toilets and onto tables and up and down stairs. Try to consider these exploits as serious experiments in your healthy child's continuing thirst and quest for learning. If you accept this behavior as his only method of learning at this age and not as "naughty" behavior or his way of upsetting you, it will prevent a good deal of trouble, both for you and for your child. Two more examples should illustrate what I mean.

Mother No. 1 reported what her fifteen-month-old had just done to her. "Dr. Eden, Joseph just crawled into the living room and smashed my most expensive piece of glassware. I am sure he did it to get even with me." Mother No. 2 informed me that her seventeen-month-old boy just climbed out of his crib for the first time. "Dr. Eden, wasn't that a fantastic accomplishment? I am so proud of him." All things being equal, Jimmy, who was lucky enough to have mother No. 2, has a much better chance of developing to his full potential.

It's easier said than done, but try to keep your "no's" down to a minimum. As one mother recently told me, "I'm doing much better. I'm pretty sure I went through an entire day with less than one hundred no's." Save your no's for the important times, such as when he's around hot stoves or open windows. If you say no to every minor infraction of the rules, your baby is less likely to pay attention to you when it really counts.

During this time you will probably notice that your child is starting "make believe" behavior, such as talking into a toy telephone or pretending to drive a toy truck. Our son was an avid transportation enthusiast at this age. He would drive all sorts of toy cars and trucks for hours on end each day. He is now all grown up and still involved in transportation, but now he pilots a real airplane.

Many twelve- to eighteen-month-olds begin to show preference for one hand over the other. I would strongly advise that you not interfere in any way and not encourage using the right hand over the left. For those of you who hope that your child grows up to be a champion tennis player, this suggestion is easy to follow. After all, Rod Laver and Jimmy Connors are both left-handed and it has not hurt their careers in the slightest. On the contrary, it probably gives them an advantage. For what it is worth, I am also left-handed. Forcing a naturally left-handed person to change may lead to learning, speech, and writing problems later on. So simply let nature take its course.

Before we move on to the growth and development charts, let me emphasize that although it will be more work for you, try to give your baby the benefit of the doubt as he roams about. He must be allowed to begin to tear loose from you and become more independent and self-sufficient. He must be allowed to explore and learn, since pride in achievement is essential for his future well-being. You should take a balanced approach in your parenting. By this I mean that you should not put too much emphasis on one particular area. Rather, give equal time and effort to his physical, emotional, and mental development. Most important, don't try to push him too hard or too fast. Each child develops at a different rate and no two are alike. All you have to do is love him and trust him. The time you spend with him should be quality time. Show him you're on his side and give him the space, opportunity, and tools to be active and happy.

## 12 – 18 Months

## GROWTH AND DEVELOPMENT
*Physical (Motor)*

### 12 – 15 months

1. Walks with slight support or walks alone.
2. Climbs onto low chairs and sofas.
3. Skillful pincer movements of thumb and index finger.
4. Can usually build two- to three-block towers.
5. Proficient in removing small objects from receptacles.
6. Can sometimes climb stairs while standing and holding on, and often on hands and knees.
7. Enjoys feeding himself; usually holds and handles spoon and cup.
8. Can unscrew tops of cans and can turn doorknobs.
9. Enjoys sitting on floor and pivoting around while at play.

### 15 – 18 months

1. Walks well, trots, and begins to run.
2. Can scribble with a pencil or crayon.
3. Fine stairway climber.
4. Can stand on one foot and can walk backwards.
5. Can build three- to four-block towers.
6. May climb out of crib.
7. Throws ball with enthusiasm but with little control.
8. Walks along with pull toys.
9. Can turn pages of book, usually more than one page at a time.
10. Begins to show hand preference.

*Note:* These charts are based on average *ranges* of growth and development; many normal babies perform and achieve either sooner or later than indicated.

## 12 – 18 Months

## GROWTH AND DEVELOPMENT
*Emotional (Social)*

### 12 – 15 months

1. Shows affection.

2. Fine sense of humor, laughs heartily.
3. Loves audiences and demands attention.
4. More self-assertive and stubborn and may show signs of temper and temper tantrums.
5. Begins to show real negative behavior.
6. Rapid mood shifts.
7. Loves to imitate, especially doing housework.
8. Upset with separation from familiar people; prefers certain people over others.

### 15 – 18 months

1. Starts to say no.
2. Willful, stubborn, negative, with or without temper tantrums.
3. Becoming less afraid of strangers.
4. Still demands attention.
5. Aware and sensitive to the emotions of parents; sometimes can be cooperative; e.g., hands certain objects to parents; waves bye-bye on request.

*Note:* These charts are based on average *ranges* of growth and development; many normal babies perform and achieve either sooner or later than indicated.

## 12 – 18 Months

### GROWTH AND DEVELOPMENT
*Mental (Intellectual)*

### 12 – 15 months

1. Begins to use language; says up to six meaningful words.
2. Understands and responds to some words and some short phrases.
3. Jabbers and babbles with expression.
4. Responds and comes when called.
5. Imitates simple acts, such as household chores.
6. Can fit blocks into appropriate-sized openings.
7. Can find and bring back an object that is hidden.
8. Is able to point to familiar objects and people when asked.
9. Can look at pictures in a book with understanding.
10. Enjoys taking off some of his clothes.
11. May be able to make his wishes known by gestures and voice expressions.

95

## 15 – 18 months

1. Meaningful vocabulary, sometimes up to 10 words or more, and a couple of 2-word phrases such as "bye-bye" and "all gone."
2. Great increase in understanding words and phrases; responds to questions and follows simple commands.
3. Calls himself by name, and his favorite word is "no."
4. Excellent ability to imitate words without necessarily knowing their meaning.
5. Very proficient at imitating adults' behavior and actions.
6. Can point to different parts of his body on request.
7. Can handle a crayon or pencil fairly well; usually scribbles but may occasionally draw a relatively straight line.
8. Can put simple puzzles together.
9. Avid explorer, especially of drawers, wastepaper baskets, and toilet bowls.

*Note:* These charts are based on average *ranges* of growth and development; many normal babies perform and achieve either sooner or later than indicated.

## PHYSICAL (MOTOR) DEVELOPMENT

### NUTRITION

The decrease in appetite seen in some nine- to twelve-month-olds may be even more dramatic during the twelve- to eighteen-month period. Many babies at this age become choosy and finicky eaters and develop distinct food dislikes as well as preferences. There are days when they eat next to nothing. If you can accept this as normal behavior and if you believe me when I tell you that your child won't starve or waste away if he skips a few meals, you and your toddler will have less trouble during mealtimes.

If you are still breast feeding your baby and both of you are happy with it, there is no reason to stop. The fact is that by this time most mothers have gotten their babies off the breast. By one year of age, babies can safely be started on whole cow's milk. Those babies who have been fed formula up to now also can be switched to cow's milk.

**Myth:** *Every child needs to drink one quart of milk per day.* This belief is wonderful for the dairy industry, but there really is no valid medical or nutritional reason for a child to drink a quart each day. All of us, including toddlers and children, can get along very well on considerably less. Two glasses of milk per day (a total of sixteen ounces) are

enough to satisfy all your child's needs, including his calcium requirements. If your baby enjoys drinking milk, let him have as much as he
wants, as long as you do not exceed one quart per day. Drinking much
more than that will probably interfere with his appetite for solid foods,
which can lead to iron-deficiency anemia.

Your toddler should be continued on the well-balanced, nutritious
diet that was outlined in the previous chapter. Most babies can now be
given a diet consisting of regular table foods and can eat alongside the
rest of the family. Many enjoy feeding themselves and become pretty
skillful in handling a spoon and cup. Some need more help than others.
There are those children who still prefer strained baby foods and reject
the lumpier table foods. If this is the case, it is perfectly acceptable to
continue to feed your child baby foods. Offer him a varied diet, including plenty of fruit and vegetables. Stay away from so-called "junk"
foods as much as possible. The subject of snacks will be discussed in the
next chapter.

Mealtimes should be pleasant and relaxed — but sad to say, often
they're just the opposite. Decreased appetite, negative behavior, and
overactivity can easily lead to chaos in the kitchen. If you want you child
to learn eventually to eat a sensible, well-balanced, and nutritious diet,
don't make his life miserable by forcing him to eat when he is not hungry. This is one recommendation that in my experience many parents
find difficult to accept. I probably spend more time talking to parents
about not forcing food than about any other one subject, although I
must admit that discussions related to the excretory functions of the
baby run a close second. There is more and more evidence proving
how important a well-balanced diet is for the future physical well-being
of the child. Eating habits are learned early, so this is the time to establish sound eating practices.

With table foods taking the place of strained baby foods, this is the
time to discuss salt and sugar in some detail. As I mentioned earlier, the
leading baby-food manufacturers have eliminated adding salt to all their
products and sugar to all but a few. You should do the same. Make
certain not to use added salt and sugar when cooking and preparing
table foods for your baby. If he is raised on a diet that is high in sugar
and salt, he will quickly learn to enjoy these tastes and will surely grow
up continuing to eat the same way. Let me repeat that babies are not
born craving salt or sugar. These preferences are acquired. The fact is
that a diet high in salt and sugar (and a diet high in cholesterol and
saturated fats, which will be discussed later on) starts the child on the
road to heart disease.

It is estimated that the average person in the United States consumes twelve grams of salt per day, which is many times the recommended daily requirement. You may well be inadvertently starting your baby on a diet that is too high in salt when you introduce him to table foods. Too many mothers add more salt than necessary during cooking, and add even more at the table. What happens is that you prejudge your child's food-taste preferences and use your own taste buds to decide how the food should taste. I'm the perfect example of a "salt freak," and this dates back to my early childhood. My mother used to bribe me with salty foods such as olives and pickles to get me to eat my oatmeal. She later told me that since she always loved salt, she assumed that I would also. As of today, although I know better, I sprinkle salt on my hot cereal and, as a matter of fact, on almost anything I eat. You will be doing your child a great disservice if you get him used to extra salt. There is sufficient natural salt in foods for your baby's needs. The evidence is clear that too much salt can lead to high blood pressure and kidney disease later on, or it can aggravate or enhance the problem if a familial or underlying tendency to hypertension is present.

If your baby becomes accustomed to a lot of sugar, I can guarantee you that he will always crave it. It is frightening to think about it, but according to the latest estimate, the average United States citizen swallows 102 pounds of sugar per year. The less sugar you add to the foods you feed your baby, the better. There is plenty of natural sugar in our foods, so from the nutritional point of view it is not necessary to add any more. Toddlers raised on a diet without added sugar become accustomed to such a diet and enjoy and thrive on it. Besides extra unnecessary calories which can cause obesity, excess sugar promotes dental decay. Of even greater significance in terms of the long-range physical well-being of your child is the evidence that a too-high sugar intake may contribute to the future development of heart disease. The reason is that refined sugars tend to increase the triglyceride (fat) level in the blood, which is one of the risk factors involved in developing coronary heart disease. Babies learn by example, so it would be best if you also cut down on the amount of salt and sugar you use. If you can do so, there is an extra added bonus. Your own health is bound to improve on such a diet.

A final point about nutrition. A baby normally triples his birth weight by one year of age. For example, a seven-pound newborn should weigh about twenty-one pounds at one year. If your baby has considerably more than tripled his birth weight, he may well be too fat. If this is the case, it would be a good idea to check it out with your baby's doctor, who might choose to take certain steps to slow down your baby's weight gain. Being fat is not healthy at any age.

These little dynamos, with few exceptions, are naturally superactive and more than ready for any and all physical activity. They require the space and opportunity and need the proper toys and materials to develop both their small and large muscles to the fullest. For the first time, the purchase of some special equipment is useful, but elaborate and expensive paraphernalia is not necessary.

The following are my specific suggestions for helping to develop your baby's coordination, strength, and muscles.

**Push and pull toys.** By this I mean toys such as cars and trucks. These are great fun and give your child the opportunity to move around in his make-believe world. Many of these push and pull toys have noises built in to function as they move, and the sound effects make the activity even more pleasurable. These toys are useful for both small- and large-muscle development.

**Balls.** Let your child take the lead in playing with balls of various sizes. Some babies this age learn to throw a ball, but it is a bit too soon for you to try to teach him to pitch to a target. Footballs and Ping-Pong balls seem to be particularly useful.

**Crawling games.** Anything you can figure out that will make crawling fun for your baby is splendid exercise for his large muscles. One example would be a large cardboard box such as the box a television set comes in. Simply cut out the sides, and presto — he has an indoor or outdoor playhouse.

**Small-muscle activities.** 1) Hammering toys: These are noisy but necessary. Your child learns dexterity and becomes better coordinated while having a great time pounding away.

2) Beads for stringing: Large wooden beads on a thick string are fine. By around eighteen months of age most toddlers are ready to play with beads.

3) Plastic snap-lock rings: These are made to be pulled apart and snapped together. Your child can spend many happy hours practicing this new skill.

**Roughhouse activities.** No special equipment is needed except a soft enough floor (put down a blanket or pad) or a bed. The more of these activities, the better, not only for his overall physical development but for his emotional well-being as well. The wrestling match should be interrupted frequently for rest periods and for large hugs.

*Chase him and catch him games.* There is little question that you will get tired of these games sooner than your child will.

*Hide-and-seek games.* This type of game still is a favorite.

*Outdoor play yard.* Having your own or a neighbor's yard is ideal, but if it's not available, it is no great tragedy. A playground with the proper equipment is just as good, but in some neighborhoods such a facility is hard to find. Weather permitting, get your baby outside as often as possible. There are several types of outdoor yard play that children especially enjoy.

They love playing in a sandbox filled with plenty of dirt (be sure it is not combined with dog or cat feces) and the proper utensils (cups, spoons, balls, funnels, and strainers). A lot of dirt is the key. I once talked to a mother of an eighteen-month-old boy whose greatest pleasure in life was rolling around in the dirt. Mrs. F. happened to be a fastidious lady who could not stand seeing Johnny dirty and so she took him out of his natural habitat every hour on the hour. She would drag him screaming and yelling into the house to give him a bath and then take him back to his sandbox. All I can say is that this little guy was pretty water-logged by dinnertime.

**Myth:** *Dirt is unhealthy for a child.* Nothing could be further from the truth. There is nothing dangerous about dirt as long as it is not mixed with animal feces. A bath before dinner after a whole day of wallowing in dirt is sufficient.

Children also enjoy playing on climbing equipment. This is a real luxury but can be used well beyond eighteen months of age. There are a number of different types of climbing equipment on the market. A low-to-the-ground jungle gym is one. Another is a dome climber, based on the geodesic principle of construction developed by the famous Buckminster Fuller. It is sturdy and can hold as many kids as can climb on it at a given time. The dome climber should be set up on either grass or sand to soften and cushion any possible falls. It is well-constructed and can last and give good service throughout the entire preschool period. It furnishes fine exercise and also builds up your baby's self-confidence as he becomes a more and more proficient climber. The dome climber has another function: if it is covered with canvas, it instantly converts to a tent or fort.

If you have a yard, your child will also like water play. All you need is a plastic basin and some plastic toys. The important thing to remember is to keep the water level no higher than four inches. I would advise that this activity always be supervised.

**Indoor climber and slide.** There are a number of these on the market. If you have the room and resources, one of these can function as an excellent source of good exercise and play when weather or circumstances do not permit you to go outside with your baby.

Let me close this section by reminding you that plenty of fresh air is healthy for your child. Get him outside every chance you get. Even if he has a simple cold but is acting normally, there is no reason to keep him indoors. If he has a full-blown upper respiratory infection, it would be unfair to have him play with other children because he can spread his cold to them, but the outdoor air won't hurt him at all. Speaking of colds, here is another widely believed old wives' tale.

**Myth:** *Washing a child's hair or giving him a bath while he has a cold will cause pneumonia.* There is no truth to this. All you have to do is dry him thoroughly and then let him go about the normal business of the day.

### SAFETY TIPS

As Dr. Fitzhugh Dodson points out in his book, *How to Parent,* the key to safety at this age and beyond is to "child-proof" your apartment or house. This means making a systematic, slow, and careful trip through your entire home (including the back yard, basement, and garage if you live in a house). Try to look at things through the eyes of your toddler. Ask yourself, "Is there anything dangerous lying around that he can get hold of?" If the answer is yes, remove all such objects. A baby between twelve and eighteen months cannot be expected to differentiate between what is safe and what is unsafe. I have been involved in many toddler accidents caused entirely by not properly child-proofing the house.

**Poisons.** Many products commonly found in the house can be poisonous. Some common examples are aspirin, sleeping pills, moth balls, bleach, cosmetics, drain cleaners, and lye. The Committee on Accident and Poison Prevention of the American Academy of Pediatrics lists the following safety rules:

1. Keep dangerous products out of your child's sight and reach.
2. Take extra care during times of family stress.
3. Never call medicine "candy."
4. Buy medicine and household products in child-resistant packages and use these packages as directed. (Even these can be opened by many children.)
5. Never leave alcoholic beverages within a child's reach.
6. Seek help if your child has swallowed a nonfood substance.
7. Keep a one-ounce bottle of syrup of ipecac in your medicine cabinet. Check with your doctor as to the dosage to be used if your child accidentally swallows a poisonous substance. Syrup of ipecac induces vomiting.

You should also be aware of another type of poisoning which is caused by lead ingestion. Lead sources are everywhere in our environment. Paint is still by far the most common source of lead in the urban United States. Before 1950, most houses were painted both inside and outside with paint containing large amounts of lead. Many of these homes, which have now deteriorated, are particularly dangerous since the lead paint can be inhaled in the form of dust; also, some children eat the paint as it chips. In 1973, the United States Federal Government forbade the sale via interstate commerce of paint containing more than 0.5 percent lead. Nevertheless, there are still many houses with high-content-lead paint still on their walls. Plaster containing lead is also a common source. According to the 1970 census, 30 million such dwellings are still in use, about one-quarter of which are in debilitated condition. If you live in such a house, I would advise that you immediately take the necessary precautions to eliminate this potentially serious poison. Lead poisoning can cause severe, irreversible brain damage to a child. Be especially careful if your child is in the habit of eating nonfood substances (called pica).

*Falls and cuts.* Always remember that doors and screens at stairways, doorways, and other dangerous areas should be safely fastened. Use plastic dishes and cups. Try to remove furniture with sharp edges and use nonskid mats in the bathtub. I would suggest that you install appropriate guards on all windows, especially above the ground floor.

*Drowning.* Never leave your child alone in water (whether he's in the bathtub or elsewhere) since even shallow water is dangerous. You must always accompany your child to a pool or lake.

*Automobile safety.* Never allow your child to play alone in the driveway or in the car. Place safety latches on your car doors. While the car is in motion, always use an approved child safety car restraint or seat.

***Hearing.*** The following is a possible danger signal pointing to a hearing difficulty: a twelve-month-old who does not start to imitate the sounds that his parents make to him. If this is a problem with your baby, consult your physician.

## EMOTIONAL (SOCIAL) DEVELOPMENT

I will start this section by listing some of the expected character traits of your twelve- to eighteen-month-old. With these in mind you will be in a stronger position to continue to help your baby develop the emotional stability and positive self-image so essential for his future well-being. You can look forward to:

1. Negative behavior
2. Impulsiveness
3. Self-assertion
4. Independence
5. Selfishness and stubbornness
6. Demands for attention
7. Rapid mood changes
8. Sense of humor
9. Affectionate behavior

As you can see, your work is cut out for you. How you handle your child during these six months will either prepare him to cope with the outside world with optimism and enthusiasm or will reduce his chances of growing up happy, secure, and self-reliant.

The question as to whether a mother should or should not go back to work often comes up around this time. This is an extremely important decision and requires careful thought and consideration. The question cannot be answered with a simple yes or no. It all depends on the particular needs and circumstances of each individual family.

### THE MOTHER'S RETURN TO WORK

There are three basic reasons why a mother chooses to go back to work rather than stay home to care for her baby: economic demands, preference, and outside pressures.

***Economic demands.*** Opinion polls have shown that this is the main reason mothers go back to work. Over one-half of the women who work state that if they had the choice, they would prefer to stay home. The economics of life today force many women back into the job market. Many families just cannot make ends meet without two paychecks.

**Preference.** Some mothers prefer to pursue a career outside the house rather than being content with a career as a mother and homemaker. It makes little sense to me to force such a mother to remain at home by instilling guilt rather than allowing her to "do her thing." A discontented, depressed mother who would rather be out working but stays home instead will feel that the world is passing her by. Such a woman will not be able to give enough of herself to satisfy her baby's emotional needs. This type of mother may provide full-time care for her child, but this does not necessarily mean that this mother will provide full maternal quality care.

**Outside pressures.** It has been my experience that some women go back to work even though they actually would prefer staying home and being full-time mothers. At a cocktail party, some mothers are actually embarrassed to say that they are "only" housewives and mothers, and this is unfortunate. The so-called career woman who looks down her nose at the mother who chooses to stay home to devote herself to her baby has a lot to learn about life. This outside pressure is the wrong reason to go back to work. Rather than being embarrassed about choosing to stay home, such mothers should be proud to take on what I consider the most important job of their life, the job of full-time mother.

At last count, over one-third of women who have children under six years of age are working, so if you must or prefer to work, you will have plenty of company. The lack of well-run and well-staffed child-care services that are reasonably priced is a "source of constant stress" for all women studied, regardless of economic level, according to a recent Columbia University study entitled "Parenting in an Unresponsive Society." The important question here is, what happens to the children of working mothers? In my experience and in the experience of others, the children of working mothers do just as well as those of nonworking mothers, provided the proper mother surrogate or group-care facility is found. Unfortunately, this is easier said than done. A baby needs loving and intimate care and not simply a baby sitter who satisfies his physical needs. In his recent book *The Growth of the Child* the noted psychologist Dr. Jerome Kagan poses the question, "Do infants attending a well-run, responsible group-care center five days a week during the first two years of life display different patterns of psychological development

**105**

compared with infants of the same sex and family background who are being reared in a typical nuclear family?" The results of his investigation showed that children from intact and psychologically supportive families who experience surrogate care during the first two years of life resemble home-reared children from the same social and ethnic group. No significant changes in psychological and social development were noted between both groups. His conclusion was that a group-care environment, if properly run, does not alter the effects on the child of his home environment. To quote from Dr. Kagan, "A family has a mysterious power which is perhaps one reason why it has been the basic and most stable unit in this and other societies for so long a time." To this I say, "amen."

How old should the baby be before the mother goes back to work? There is no specific magic age. I have a lawyer friend who went back to work when her baby was two weeks old and everything turned out fine. This new mother was lucky to have access to a great mother of her own. Grandma did a beautiful job during her daughter's working hours. Most families are not so fortunate and have a frustrating and difficult time looking for the proper mother substitute or group-care facility. Until you find one, make every effort to stay with your baby.

Except for the group of mothers who have no choice and must of economic necessity go back to work, there is a trade-off that you must carefully consider as you decide whether or not you want to do so. You must weigh the guilt and fatigue and worry you feel about the possible adverse effects on your baby versus the self-fulfillment and satisfaction you derive from working in the outside world. What is needed above everything else is a relaxed, happy, loving household, and whatever route you decide to take in order to better achieve that goal is the right one.

The ideal situation in terms of the emotional development of a baby is to be born to a mother who is not forced to go back to work for economic reasons and who prefers to stay home with her child. If such a mother spends the baby's first three years as a full-time mother happy to provide loving and stimulating care, the chances of raising an emotionally sound and stable child are great.

### SPECIFIC RECOMMENDATIONS

The following are the specific activities, toys, and approaches that I believe will encourage your toddler to develop the positive social characteristics that you would like to see.

***Other children.*** It is a good idea at this point to start inviting other children close to your baby's age into your house, as well as to take your baby out to the park so that he can establish contact with his peers. Your baby needs the company of other children, and this will better prepare him for future nursery school and preschool experiences.

***Sharing.*** Although the twelve- to eighteen-month-old is basically rather selfish, it is nevertheless important to begin to teach him what sharing is all about. You can do this alone with him but it is more effectively accomplished when other children are around. For example, with two other playmates present, bring out three of your child's toys and distribute them, one to each child, explaining what you are doing. I must admit that this does not always work out, but it's worth a try.

***Daily routine.*** Babies at this age are happy with a set routine and become confused and upset if each day is totally different from the previous day. Therefore, within limits try to establish a set daily schedule and routine. Let the baby know that it's naptime or time to put away toys for the day; he will enjoy these rituals, but you will also be helping him to acquire helpful habits.

***Consistency.*** Your approach and responses should always be consistent. Your baby will continually test you to see if you really mean what you say. There is nothing more disturbing for the child than having you say yes one time and no the next to the same request or action on his part. Both the mother and father must try to remain consistent. If not, your baby will start playing one parent against the other, and this destructive game will continue as he grows older.

***Protection versus overprotection.*** This is a tough one to handle. Overprotection will fill your child with needless fears and will hurt his self-confidence and lower his self-image. If you have adequately "child-proofed" your house, let him go and don't worry too much about his physical safety. This leads me to the subject of falls. Toddlers all fall down, usually many times each day. You can sympathize, but unless the fall is really a nasty one, my advice is not to make a big fuss. Rather than run to his aid, let your baby get up by himself. This approach will help him build up his self-confidence and independence and will reduce his overdependence on you.

***Negative behavior.*** Don't fall into the trap of responding to your toddler's anger and stubborness by screaming and yelling. Mrs. W. came to my office to ask my advice about handling Thomas's temper tantrums. "Would you believe that Tom actually screams and wildly kicks the wall when he does not get his way?" It turned out that little Tom had learned to kick walls from big Tom, his father, who, when sufficiently provoked, did exactly the same thing. Many of us forget the truism that children learn primarily by example.

Except for special occasions, such as when he's tried to climb out the window, try not to hit your baby, no matter how angry you are. I would also discourage you from yelling and threatening. The most effective way to handle your child's negative behavior is to distract him with a toy, another activity, or a change of scene. If all that does not work, I would suggest that you simply separate him from you, remaining calm and quiet as you do so. Put him in his room and explain to him that when he feels better about things, he can come back out. Toddlers are extremely sensitive to your emotions and will understand when you are disappointed in their behavior. Although they can't speak too well themselves, they have a clear understanding of what is going on around them.

**Unrealistic goals.** Do not expect or demand perfection from your baby. Rather, whenever possible, register your pride in his accomplishments. For example, if he shares his toys with a playmate, make a big fuss about it and tell him how proud you are. If he responds to one of your requests such as handing you something you ask for, give him a big kiss and a hug and tell him how happy you are that you have him. It is a two-way street: you are around to make him happy and he must also learn that he is around to make you happy.

**Exploration.** Give your child opportunities to explore and to learn. If he somehow gets his hands on one of your favorite books and tears out every single page, don't react as if this is hostile behavior on his part. Although it won't be easy, accept it as his only way of learning a new skill, part of his scientific research projects for that day.

**Rules.** At this age you should begin to teach your toddler some simple rules and routines, such as touching people gently. Again, praise him when he does follow the rules.

TOYS

**Dolls and cuddly, soft animals.** These encourage feelings of tenderness, protection, and care and so are very important. They are also

useful in helping your baby with dramatic play. He will be able to act out more easily the rules of various family members and will also be better able to play out important emotions. It's a good idea to store these dolls and large soft animals on a shelf that your child can reach by himself when he wants them.

**Myth:** *Little boys who play with dolls will turn out to be effeminate.* I am glad to say that nowadays fewer parents believe this ridiculous notion. Similarly, little girls who play with trucks don't turn out to be masculine. Little boys should be allowed to play with dolls and little girls with trucks, and in the end it all works out fine.

Mr. J. called me one morning, bitterly complaining about the doll his little boy received as a birthday present from Mr. J.'s mother-in-law. "What's she trying to do, make Mike a fairy?" I happened to be in a particularly bad mood that day, so I told him what I thought about this in rather strong terms.

**Rhythm instruments.** Drums, cymbals, tin cans, and metal pans are all useful, and your toddler will enjoy playing with them. Even though you may not appreciate the noise, it is wrong to deprive him of this pleasurable activity.

**Music.** This is a good time to start your child's record collection. Twelve- to eighteen-month-olds have broad musical tastes. They love to dance in time to the music, either by themselves or with you. They also love rhymes and jingles and are good at imitating. Incidentally, music is a fine way to improve a nasty mood.

I would be remiss if I did not warn you about an interesting trait that is common during this twelve- to eighteen-month period: sudden silence. When this happens and your toddler is not in sight, I would advise you to immediately stop what you are doing and investigate. The chances are good that he has found something extremely interesting to occupy his time. The best example that comes to mind concerned Mrs. P. She told me about her seventeen-month-old who had quietly smeared an entire living room wall with her red lipstick. "I found my little painter standing in front of the wall silently admiring his artwork with a great big smile on his face." How would you have reacted to this?

## MENTAL (INTELLECTUAL) DEVELOPMENT

During these six months your baby will make tremendous advances in his intellectual capacities. His memory is improving day by day. He imitates more and more efficiently without actually understanding the meaning of most of the words or phrases he imitates. He will become more and more interested in pictures and he will start to be able to solve simple puzzles. Most important is that his understanding of the world around him and his verbal understanding both expand enormously. It is important to remember that repetition is still the key to his learning.

As yet he probably will not be able to internalize his thinking processes. The "thoughtfulness" that is characteristic of the baby over eighteen months of age will not be seen. As Dr. Burton White points out in his excellent book, *The First Three Years of Life,* a child before eighteen months of age attempts possible solutions in the open rather than in his head. He cannot as yet "think out" possible solutions before attempting to solve the problem. Rather, he jumps right in, using trial and error rather than pausing or taking time to evaluate the situation.

These toddlers are preparing themselves for the big step forward to real "intelligence" as we usually understand it. There is much you can do during this time to help. In our society a high premium is put on academic achievement. If you are interested in having your child do as well as possible in school, these six months should be put to good use. It is not at all difficult; you do not have to be a college professor to be able to furnish your child with the activities and mental stimulation he needs to make full use of his intellectual capacity. In approaching this job it is important for you to always remember *not* to push him too hard. Each and every child develops at a different rate and in a different way. A child learns much more rapidly if he is enjoying a particular activity. These little children also have "good" days and "bad" days, just like the rest of us. If your toddler rebels or is not interested, there is no point in trying to force him to learn or perform.

The following are the activities, toys, and equipment that I believe will be most useful in helping your child develop his mental capabilities to the fullest:

### BOOKS

The sooner you expose your baby to books, the better. All educators agree that early involvement with and love of books are among the main determining factors of future excellence in school.

**Scrapbook.** I am referring to a book of your baby's own. All you need is some thick materials, such as cardboard, to use for pages, and some pictures of familiar objects. Work together with your toddler and paste these pictures onto the pages one by one. As you do it, talk to him about the meaning and characteristics of each picture. If he sometimes prefers to tear out the pages instead of pasting them in, so be it. He will be ready for pasting the next day or the next week or the next month.

**Picture books.** There are many excellent picture books that you can purchase. Dr. Seuss's *Cat in the Hat* dictionary is a favorite. With your child sitting on your lap, point to a picture and say the word. He may be able to repeat the word or he may not. After awhile, when real understanding sets in, you can ask him to find the cat or the dog, and so on. Finally, if he is a verbal type you will be able to point to a particular picture and he will say the word. This is an easy way to build up his vocabulary. Don't be discouraged if he does not actually articulate the word; this is not a sign of impaired intelligence.

Mrs. A. could not believe that her eighteen-month-old had yet to utter his first word. "What is the matter with him? He probably is not too bright," she said. On the contrary, Billy was very intelligent. He was able to point to just about everything he wanted and could understand a great many words and phrases. For example, when Billy was asked to turn on the TV set, he would walk right over and would not only turn it on, but was also able to change the channels. Incidentally, this little fellow finally started to talk when he was about two years of age, and as his mother told me later, "It's amazing. Billy started talking practically in sentences!"

**Reading.** Read aloud — Mother Goose rhymes, animal stories, and the like. An ideal time for this is at bedtime. Sharing a book with your baby sitting on your lap is a wonderful way to end each of his days. You will know soon enough if he is happy with your choice of book. I would encourage you to make this a bedtime ritual. It is something he can always look forward to. These reading sessions are of enormous benefit and will allow him to absorb much knowledge and information.

## CRAYONS

Supply your child with a batch of different-colored crayons and give him plenty of paper. The floor is probably the best place for this activity. His art will be more impressionistic than traditional, but these crayons give him a chance to develop skill and dexterity. Working with crayons will better prepare him to master the use of a pencil and pen later on.

## LANGUAGE

Verbal competence is a must for success in school. The best way to handle language is to teach your child new words that are related to his experiences. For example, if he cuts his finger and cries, tell him that the cut hurts or that he has a "boo-boo." Talk to him about what he sees, noting not only the name of the object but its size, shape, taste, and color. Speak out loud to him about what you are doing or seeing. Point to the particular object and name it. Parallel talk is an effective method of teaching language. By this I mean talking to your child about what is happening to him at the time; for example, "Joseph is eating his cereal."

Besides talking, listen together with him to what is going on, both inside and outside the house. For example, if you both hear the telephone ring, tell him that the telephone is ringing. If you both hear thunder, talk to him about the thunder. Also take the time to listen to his responses to what you say — many parents don't wait for an answer. If he responds appropriately, be sure to tell him so and show him how proud you are of his accomplishment.

Action rhymes and songs are very useful. With your toddler's increasing understanding of words and phrases, these rhymes and songs are an excellent way not only to have fun together but to teach him language and new concepts. I am sure that you are familiar with many of these. Two old-time favorites are "London Bridge Is Falling Down" and "Ring Around the Rosie."

Passive language predominates in this period of your child's life. Passive language means that he understands what is said to him. Active language or actual talking usually is only a small part of his total language development before eighteen months of age.

## TOYS AND GAMES

**Fit-together puzzles.** Use only simple puzzles having no more than three pieces. These are useful for your child's hand/eye coordination, and also help him learn to see and understand the concept of different shapes. You can make up your own fit-together puzzle by pasting a large picture on a piece of cardboard and then cutting it up into two or three pieces. Show him how to put the pieces together and then let him try. Don't be discouraged if he fails. Repeat the process, and sooner or later he will succeed. At that point he deserves a big kiss.

***Tower building.*** Wooden or plastic blocks are best for this activity. Aside from the manual dexterity your toddler will develop, these blocks will teach him to manipulate variables. As he tries to build with the blocks, he learns about different sizes and shapes, and sometimes even different colors. This is a problem-solving activity and so can help to prepare him to handle school problems later on, especially in understanding mathematics.

***Sorting games.*** There are endless possibilities for such games all around you. For example, laundry sorting is one. With your baby nearby, sort your washed, clean laundry into three separate piles, Mommy's, Daddy's, and the baby's. Explain to your child what each pile represents. Then mix them up and ask him to try to separate the clothes. Don't expect him to do a perfect job the first time around. Don't be surprised if your husband comes down to breakfast one morning wearing a size 2 toddler undershirt. Another example of a sorting game is to take two different sets of objects, such as a number of blocks and a number of balls, and show your baby how to separate them, the blocks on one side and balls on the other. This understanding of different groupings is basic to intelligence. For one thing, it will improve any I.Q. test score your toddler may take later on. Sorting and separating by group is a favorite concept used in testing intelligence.

***Chores.*** These are splendid for learning vocabulary and word meaning. As you go about washing the dishes, ask your child to please give you a towel. Then use the towel to dry the dish. Always talk to him about what you are both doing. Putting pots away, turning off the faucets, and the like are all much more interesting than just a quiz session, which will just bore him and turn him off of learning anything.

***Nesting books and stacking discs.*** There are many to choose from and they are inexpensive. These books and discs teach your toddler to sort and to put objects in order according to their size. This is useful in helping him build a foundation for mathematical thinking, and will stand him in very good stead when he starts school.

***Follow the leader.*** This activity is most effective and enjoyable when played with other children. By eighteen months of age, and sometimes a bit earlier, most toddlers are ready for this. For example, tap your head, clap your hands, touch your knees, and on and on. Ask your child and his friends to do the same. This is a good learning experience and also is an activity that allows your child to spend happy times with his colleagues.

***Touching games.*** Simply touch an object and have your child do the same. Explain what he is feeling as he touches the object — its size, shape, texture, and color. He may not yet understand all these characteristics but he will be learning all the time. Make it a game, not a test of his knowledge.

***Imitation games.*** For example, pull your ear lobe and ask your toddler to do the same to himself. He may pull your ear instead, but after some practice, most babies at this age will begin to respond appropriately. When he does succeed, he has made a large step forward in intelligence. It will mean that his mind is starting to function on a symbolic level for the very first time. Symbolic thinking means that he can now form a picture in his mind — in this case, that he knows where his ear is without actually seeing it.

***Water play.*** Since your baby probably enjoys water, it is a perfect place for him to learn. All you need are some different-sized containers. Pour water from one into the other and discuss with him what you are doing. "I am pouring the water from the little one into the big one." Then reverse the process. Next, let him try, and tell him what he is doing as he goes about pouring the water — and, of course, spilling it all over the floor.

Bath boats are also nice to have around. Let me again remind you never to leave your child alone when he is in or around water.

***Animal toys.*** It is not enough just to give your child various animal toys. You should explain something about each one. For example, a toy duck requires a "quack-quack" to go with it and a toy cat, a "meow." Then, when you're outside with your baby and happen to see a cat, point it out to your baby and say, "That is a cat. It goes 'meow-meow.'" If that particular cat has also read this book, he will promptly "meow" himself, and that will really complete this sound-effects lesson.

***Cause-and-effect (If, then) games.*** The type of thought process involved in these games is probably the most important one of all in terms of intellectual development, and is crucial for succeeding in school. You can make these games up yourself without any trouble. The purpose is to teach your child what is called relational theory: *if* you do this, *then* this will happen. Put another way, one action causes something else to happen. For example, put a toy car on a flat surface and show your baby that it does not move and that it must be pushed in order to make it go. Then put the same car on a slight incline and show him that with only a slight push, it will start rolling down the incline. Finally, put the same car on a steep incline and show him that it will roll down by itself, without being pushed. This is cause and effect, or if, then. Your child also just had a lesson in momentum — and he learned about it while he was interested and having fun.

Another example of cause and effect uses various screw-top toys or simple jars. Show your child how they work. Show him how to unscrew the top. This is another if, then activity. If he does this — in this case, turns the screw top — then this will happen: the top will come off, and he can then reach into the jar.

At this age, toddlers are eager to learn and enthusiastic, and are ready to take on many new challenges and new tasks. Make the activities pleasurable and don't overburden your child with problems that he is either uninterested in or not yet capable of solving. Finally, don't compare him to your neighbor's child, who may be further advanced in some of his exploits. Your baby will learn at his own rate, and if you give him the proper opportunities, he will ultimately reach his full potential.

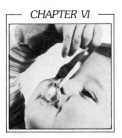

# CHAPTER VI

# Eighteen to Twenty-Four Months

## INTRODUCTION

"You know, Dr. Eden, I can almost see the little wheels turning in Amy's head. She is starting to think like a real person."

This mother was talking about her little twenty-month-old as I was preparing to give the baby an immunization injection. I might add that Amy was not only "thinking" about the needle she was about to get, but at the same time she was solving the problem she faced by running out of the examining room. Dr. Jean Piaget, the famous Swiss psychologist, one of the true pioneers in infant and early childhood development, refers to the eighteen- to twenty-four month period as the "problem-solving" stage. In the mental development section of this chapter I will discuss in some detail how babies at this age think and the

119

tremendous advances they make in their intellectual capacities if given proper stimulation and opportunity. For purposes of introduction to this subject, the key words to remember are problem solving, symbolic thinking (images and ideas in the head), increased memory span, and, of course, verbal competence.

Verbal competence, both passive and active, is probably the most dramatic and obvious advance your baby will make during these marvelous and exciting six months. By age two, most babies have a speaking vocabulary of twenty words or more, and may also properly use a few two-word sentences. More important, they will learn to understand the meaning of hundreds of different words and simple phrases. As we already have stated, verbal competence is essential for your child's future academic success, and there is much that you can do to help your baby in this particular area of her development. The more talking you do to her about the world around her, the better. The more you listen to her and respond appropriately, the greater will be her chances of mastering verbal skills to her full capacity.

You will now notice that your child begins to study and investigate the *quality* of the objects she gets her hands on. She will feel them, drop them, chew on them, look at them, and throw them. She will be fascinated by opening and closing doors and drawers. Let her explore and practice these new skills to her heart's content. Again, try to keep your "no's" down to a minimum. Make every effort not to discourage her interest and curiosity. If you fall into the trap of stopping her at every turn, you will have put a damper on her zeal and drive for learning, and this will adversely affect her later school performance. I have said it before, but let me repeat it: your baby's enthusiastic search for knowledge must be encouraged in every way possible.

It will become obvious to you that your eighteen- to twenty-four-month-old still is just as full of energy as before. With her increased motor skills in running and climbing, she is now more capable of exploring and experimenting. Accidents are part of growing up, especially during this time of her life, so let me again remind you to child-proof your house. Please remember that everything still goes into her mouth, so that accidental poisonings are common during these six months. With your child's safety in mind, arrange her environment accordingly, and then give her the space and freedom she needs in order to learn and mature. Allow her to enjoy her life to the fullest as she goes about the business of growing up.

The negative behavior patterns that no doubt have already started may well continue during this period. If you handle this aspect of your child's normal development properly, you have a better chance of looking forward to a reduction in this negative behavior by her second birthday. This reminds me of a recent incident. Mrs. B. was the proud but exhausted mother of Margaret, who not only had a mind that operated faster than her speech and emotions (which indeed is characteristic of the eighteen- to twenty-four-month-old), but also was already practically a world-class sprinter and hurdler. Most of all, however, Margaret was the classic example of a stubborn and negative-minded twenty-three-month-old. We had previously discussed Margaret's willfulness and temper tantrums and the fact that she was so easily frustrated. I kept reassuring Mrs. B. that much of this type of behavior would stop by the time Margaret reached two years of age. Mrs. B. and Margaret came to see me the day after her second birthday party. Nothing had changed. In fact, the birthday party was a complete disaster, with Margaret trying to confiscate all the toys from the rest of the children at the party and having a full-blown temper tantrum as well. All I can tell you is that Margaret is the exception; you can look forward to the fact that most children really do become less selfish, stubborn, and negative at around two years of age. I will give you my recommendations about handling negativism in the section on emotion later on in this chapter.

At this time you can anticipate the start of various fears and of nightmares. Actually, these fears — of thunder, lightning, dogs, and the like — are more of a problem after your child is two years old. As I have already mentioned, these eighteen- to twenty-four-month-olds are very easily frustrated; they know what they want to do but if they are not successful, they simply are not mature enough to cope. You should realize that this is all normal behavior. It is most important that you handle this properly and firmly but without becoming angry. If you don't properly sympathize with the many frustrations your baby faces, the result will be a decrease in her self-image and self-esteem along with the development of feelings of inferiority.

Your baby will now begin to spend more and more time in make-believe play, and you should give her the tools to do so. She will also spend more time playing by herself or enjoying the company of her friends. These activities should be encouraged since they are quite important in helping to build up her self-confidence and self-reliance. In my experience, many parents are afraid to "let go." You will not be helping your child by always being around and making everything too easy for her. Now is the time in your baby's life for you to start doing

121

some managing from the sidelines. I am not for a moment advocating that you disappear from the scene. The eighteen- to twenty-four-month-old is still both very much involved with her primary caretaker and quite dependent. The trick is to learn to strike the right balance between overinvolvement and overinterference, and uninvolvement and desertion.

Although these babies are making rapid, giant strides in developing their motor skills, verbal competence, and internal thinking and problem solving, you should be aware of the fact that they do not as yet have any concept of time (which actually does not develop much before your child is six or seven years of age). If your child is having fun, time flies; and if she is not, time drags. For example, if your child is visiting a friend and having a ball, she will not want to leave when you think it's time, not because she is mean or selfish but rather because she truly believes she has only been there for a few minutes. On the other hand, if she happens to be visiting Grandma and has been there for barely five minutes and starts to cry because she wants to leave, it is not only because she is not having a good time but also because she honestly thinks that she's already been there forever.

Let me bring up the subject of television. It is true that a few eighteen- to twenty-four-month-olds can watch some TV and find it interesting. But for all practical purposes its a waste of time for most children that age, and I would discourage any emphasis on television watching until your child reaches age two (the whole subject of television watching will be discussed in the next chapter).

Each and every day is important in your child's growth. Your child is more than ready to practice her increasing skills — motor, verbal, and mental. It's a shame if any of these are slowed down during this most important stage of her development. It is also important for you to keep in mind that her personality is being shaped day by day, in large measure by how she is being treated.

To sum up, I would advise that you make every effort to watch your child in action as carefully as possible and listen to her as she goes about her daily tasks. If you are properly attuned to your baby, you will soon realize that she can often "tell" you, without using the actual words, exactly how she feels and what she needs. As Dr. Burton White points out in *The First Three Years of Life,* a *balanced* approach is what is needed at this age — and, as a matter of fact, at any age. I agree completely with him that parents who concentrate too much effort and time, for example, on verbal competence at the expense of physical development and nutrition are making a serious mistake. As you surely must have noticed by now, each chapter in this book places equal emphasis on the physical, mental, and emotional development of the child; similarly, each of these areas requires your *equal* attention. A relaxed approach is most effective. Laughing with your child and having fun with her is without question the best way to raise her. Too many parents take the job too seriously and seem to forget about their own as well as their child's sense of humor. Babies are funny, and at this age already have developed a fine sense of humor. If given half a chance they laugh a lot, and despite their many frustrations and anxieties, have a marvelous, happy time of it. In terms of the future, a happy child develops to her full potential much more easily than a child raised in a house without laughter.

## 18 – 24 Months

### GROWTH AND DEVELOPMENT
*Physical (Motor)*

1. Walks up and down stairs.
2. Runs well and usually can stop short without falling on face.
3. Skillful and adventuresome climber.
4. Can build towers of up to 5 or 6 blocks.
5. Kicks balls.
6. Throws balls, occasionally toward target.
7. Usually begins to prefer one hand over the other.
8. Learns to turn pages, one at a time.
9. Scribbles with crayon or pencil.
10. Dances to music.
11. Feeds herself efficiently using spoon and cup (can even handle peeling a banana).
12. Does everything as fast as possible; e.g., running, eating, climbing, emptying drawers.

*Note:* These charts are based on average *ranges* of growth and development; many normal babies perform and achieve either sooner or later than indicated.

## 18 – 24 Months

### GROWTH AND DEVELOPMENT
*Emotional (Social)*

1. May begin having nightmares during sleep.
2. The real start of make-believe play.
3. Easily frustrated.
4. Stubborn; wants her own way.
5. Involved in negative behavior but still enjoys pleasing others.
6. Demands attention.
7. Enjoys changes of environment and scenery.
8. Helps with chores around the house with enthusiasm and energy.
9. May develop fears; e.g., of water, dogs, thunder, or lightning.
10. Displays selfish behavior; possessive of her toys and belongings.
11. Behavior becomes better and better organized.
12. Plays well with other children (usually around her 2nd birthday).
13. Her two favorite words are "no" and "mine."
14. May start to know when bowel movement is about to happen.

*Note:* These charts are based on average *ranges* of growth and development; many normal babies perform and achieve either sooner or later than indicated.

## 18 – 24 Months

### GROWTH AND DEVELOPMENT
*Mental (Intellectual)*

1. Learns to draw a line or a circle with crayon after proper instruction.
2. Understands and follows simple instructions.
3. Points to appropriate picture in book when asked.
4. Develops usable vocabulary of up to twenty words and a few short phrases; e.g., "Mama go bye-bye."
5. Listens to and enjoys simple stories.
6. Can point to and name different parts of her body.
7. Tells you what she wants, with either gestures or words.
8. Fits various puzzles together.
9. Refers to herself by name.
10. Matches similar objects and groups of objects.
11. Helps undress herself.

**12.** Spends long periods of time just observing or staring (she's "thinking").

**13.** The start of "symbolic thinking" and "thoughtfulness."

**14.** Problem-solving capacity increases day by day.

*Note:* These charts are based on average *ranges* of growth and development; many normal babies perform and achieve either sooner or later than indicated.

## PHYSICAL (MOTOR) DEVELOPMENT

### NUTRITION

In all likelihood your baby will now be drinking cow's milk, either from a bottle or from a cup. For those few mothers who are still breast feeding, there is still no reason to stop. If both you and your baby are still enjoying the breast-feeding experience, then by all means continue it. You will find that your child will usually "tell" you one way or another when she has finally had enough of breast feeding. Each example that I have included in the book thus far is true, including the following, which you really may find hard to believe. Mrs. S. was a relaxed and loving mother who was having a marvelous time breast feeding Carole, a delightful, happy, friendly, and, at two years of age, very verbal child. When Carole was fifteen months old I asked Mrs. S. if she planned to stop breast feeding soon. "Absolutely not; why should I?" she answered. I certainly had no objection to her continuing to breast feed, and for the next two well-baby visits, at eighteen months and twenty-one months of age, I did not bring up the subject. At each of these visits Mrs. S. informed me that she was still breast feeding her daughter and that everything was fine. At the two-year-old visit the first words out of Mrs. S.'s mouth were, "Dr. Eden, I've stopped breast feeding. Would you believe that last week right in the middle of a feeding, Carole suddenly stopped, turned her head away from the breast, made a face, and told me, 'Wan' chocolate milk.'"

As I outlined in the previous chapter, babies over one year of age no longer require large quantities of milk each day. If your child drinks anywhere from twelve to sixteen ounces of milk per day, this is sufficient for her nutritional needs, as long as, in addition, she is offered the well-balanced diet that we also presented earlier. These eighteen- to twenty-four-month-olds handle a spoon and cup extremely well and usually can feed themselves without any difficulty. In addition to handling the spoon and cup, they can do even more — for example, peeling a banana. I would discourage you from getting into the habit of force-

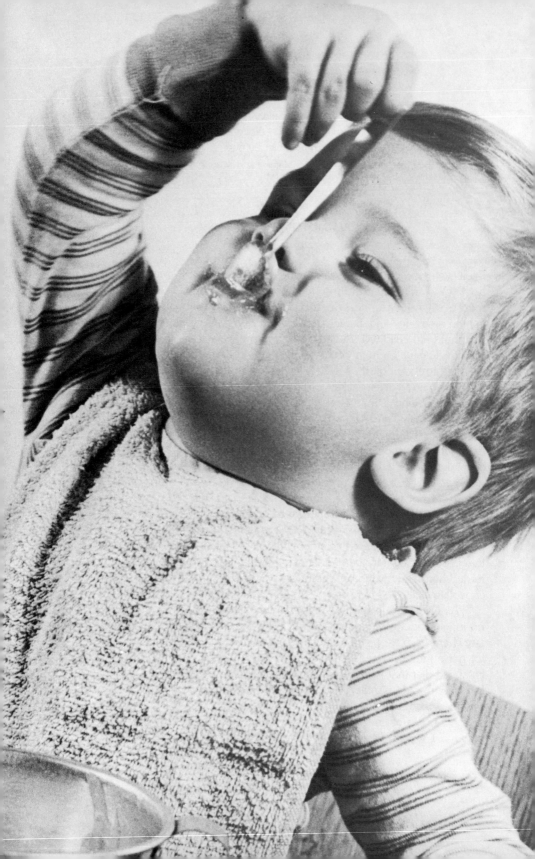

feeding your baby when and if she doesn't clean her plate. I would also advise you not to coax, cajole, threaten, or offer her a reward to get her to complete her meal. I have mentioned this before but let me repeat it: allow your child to end the meal when she thinks it's over rather than when you think she has eaten enough.

I am often asked about the amounts of various foods a child should eat. There is no specific answer to that question. Each and every baby has different requirements, a different appetite, and a different point of satiation. What I can tell you is that I have rarely seen a mother underfeed her baby. Rather, the opposite is usually the case. A little child does not need as many calories as an adult, and the child's portions of food should be smaller than your own. I must admit that there are exceptions. A certain percentage of babies have voracious appetites and they eat just about anything and everything you put in front of them. We will be discussing this subject and the whole subject of establishing proper eating patterns in the next chapter (two to three years of age). One point that I would like to make now is that it is a good idea to offer your child relatively small portions at each meal. If she is still hungry after finishing, she will tell you, and you can then replenish her plate. This is a much more sensible approach than to load up her dish with huge quantities of food that she surely should not and cannot finish. This one simple piece of advice will go a long way in starting to instill proper eating behavior. If you start this eating pattern early, the chances are that it will remain with her as she grows up and will surely result in increased health and vitality in the future.

We have already discussed how babies develop tastes for certain foods. They learn to like what you offer them; it is really as simple as that. If you offer your baby plenty of fruits, vegetables, yogurt, and the like, she will continue to enjoy these nutritious foods as she grows older. On the other hand, if you start giving her a steady diet of soda, cookies, and candy, she will grow up craving this type of junk food and will continue to eat that way all her life. Don't be afraid to offer a variety of different nutritious foods. That is the only way she will learn to eat and enjoy the well-balanced diet that is so important for her future wellbeing.

My advice is not to allow yourself to fall into the trap of appeasing and bribing your child with junk foods. Snacking between meals is fine, but it depends on what kind of snacks you use. Unfortunately, the usual between-meal foods are low in nutritive value and too high in calories and refined sugar (more about this when we take up the subject of television in the next chapter). Some excellent snacks that should always be available for your baby are plain yogurt, carrots, pieces of apple and cheese, and natural fruit juice. Please take my word for it: if you consistently offer your child this type of snack between meals instead of junk food, she will quickly learn to love it and ask for it. I would also avoid excessively salty snacks, such as salted peanuts and pretzels. In terms of her future physical health, developing correct eating patterns now is essential.

You must continue to remain on the alert for obesity. If your baby looks fat, call it to her doctor's attention. It is less likely that she will become too fat if you are careful in terms of the size of the portions and the selection of the between-meal snacks you offer her. An incredible statistic is that, in the United States, between 30 and 50 percent of all the calories eaten each day are consumed in the form of between-meal snacks. It is a fact that a fat child is not a healthy child, and this holds true from infancy through adolescence.

In the next chapter I will discuss the so-called "prudent" type of diet that I recommend for all children over two years of age. For now, I would encourage you to continue to keep the number of eggs you feed your baby down to three to four per week and continue to cut down on added salt and sugar. Offer your baby chicken, veal, and fish more often than the red and fatty meats such as pork and beef.

To close this section on nutrition for the eighteen- to twenty-four-month-old, I'd like to remind you that mealtimes can and should be fun. Try very hard to make your child's mealtimes happy experiences. This is easier said than done, but it is very important to make the attempt. You should be relaxed and cheerful as you offer your youngster a well-balanced, variety-filled, and nutritious diet. In such an environment your child will begin to associate this healthy diet more easily with good feelings all around. Such a pleasant eating environment is more conducive for your child's continuing to eat the same foods as she grows up. It is much easier to establish proper eating patterns early in life than it is to try to modify them later on.


EXERCISE

Your child's normal energy levels are such that there is very little you need to do to insure that she exercises sufficiently. If we could only figure out a way to harness all this energy, we would put the OPEC countries out of business. Eighteen- to twenty-four-month-olds run and jump and climb and have developed excellent muscle coordination. Your child will learn to kick and throw a ball and will maneuver up and down the stairs without much difficulty. If you do not put insurmountable roadblocks in her way because you are afraid of accidents, she will take care of most of her exercise requirements all by herself.

Before listing my specific recommendations for physical activities during this period, I want to caution you against using your television set as a method of keeping your child quiet and in one place. Many parents unconsciously encourage the start of a sedentary lifestyle in their children by sitting them down in front of the TV set, usually armed with cookies and candy. I suggested earlier that most eighteen- to twenty-four-month-olds do not appreciate or learn very much from TV, but still, if your child's dish is continuously replenished with goodies as she sits there, she will in short order learn to enjoy this time-wasting inactivity. This can be the start of a vicious cycle resulting in a child becoming too fat and flabby and losing all desire to be active. I am not advocating that you never put your child in front of the television set. I am suggesting that television watching and snacking be kept down to the barest minimum. At this age it is much healthier if you do not "force" your child to sit in one place for long periods of time or bribe her to do so with junk foods.

## SPECIFIC RECOMMENDATIONS

The specific suggestions that I believe will insure that your child develops to her maximum physical capacity during this period are by and large the same activities listed in the previous chapter. There are some changes in emphasis and degree of sophistication. Except for a four-wheeled vehicle of one kind or another, little additional equipment need be purchased during these six months.

**Push and pull toys.** These are still very enjoyable; in fact, they are probably more fun now, as your child really is involved in make-believe play, is more coordinated, and has more skill in handling them.

**Balls.** The games that you can play with your child at this age are more advanced and sophisticated than before. One activity that I remember enjoying with each of my children was sitting on the floor with our feet touching, and rolling a large, light ball back and forth. As we pushed the ball back and forth I talked about what we were doing: "Robert, your turn. Good. Now Daddy's turn." These ball games advanced from rolling to throwing the ball, and finally, to learning how to catch it. My daughter, Liz, enjoyed kicking the ball most and so we improvised a soccer type of game on the rug (after making sure that anything breakable was safely put away).

Games involving balls of various sizes and shapes can be played with more than one child at a time and can be a source of great pleasure for your child and her friends. Her coordination, muscle tone, strength, and agility all are helped by such activities. This is very important for her future, not only in terms of improved physical health and vigor but also in terms of improved self-image and self-confidence. Physical exercises and the acquisition of physical skills help to develop a positive body image (this subject will be discussed more fully in the next chapter).

**Crawling games.** Although your child is now standing and walking and running more and more of the time, she still enjoys crawling around. Encourage her to do so with various rug games.

**Pounding bench.** There are a number of these on the market. They usually include a hammer and large pegs and a bench. Hammering the pegs into the bench is fine for hand/eye coordination and also serves to increase muscle strength. When your child learns to hammer the pegs in efficiently, she will feel very proud of herself, and you should tell her how proud you are of her accomplishment.

**Roughhouse activities.** Continue your roughhouse activities — and don't leave out the girls.

**Myth:** *Little girls are more fragile and delicate, and weaker than little boys.* Nonsense! An eighteen- to twenty-four-month-old girl is just as strong, sturdy, and active as a boy of that age. I recall a twenty-month-old little girl whose greatest pleasure in life was wrestling with her older brother and her father. Mr. T. called me up one day to ask me about this. "Is this kind of rough exercise good for Cathy?" My answer was an emphatic, "Yes." Both boys and girls should be encouraged in every way possible to participate in vigorous and rigorous physical activity. Starting such activity at this very young age does much to insure that they will continue on the road to a lifestyle that includes taking proper care of and developing pride in their bodies.

**Outdoor play yard or park.** This was discussed in the previous chapter. Obviously it is very important that your child continue to engage in these outdoor activities. I would just like to add that if you have not yet purchased some type of climbing equipment for your child, this would be a good time to do so. The eighteen- to twenty-four-month-old is fascinated by climbing and is becoming more and more skillful at it.

**Four-wheeled vehicle.** A number of styles are available. Your child can sit on or straddle the vehicle and maneuver herself around on it. This is great exercise, and also serves to prepare your child for her first tricycle. Very few children are really ready for a tricycle much before two years of age, so I would advise you not to buy one yet.

**Chores.** In the previous chapter, chores were discussed in the section on mental development. I am including chores in the physical development section of this chapter for a specific reason. An eighteen- to twenty-four-month-old is quite strong, and willing and able to work. Therefore, it is good practice to get your child involved now in helping around the house. This will help her physical development as well as help to instill a sense of cooperation in her. I am referring to carrying out garbage, moving small pieces of furniture, carrying packages, and running to call another member of the family to the phone. All these chores are well within her physical capabilities. They are good exercise and useful as well. If you think about it, there is nothing a preschool or school teacher appreciates more than a child willing and able to cooperate and help in the classroom. Keep this fact in mind as you involve your youngster with various household chores.

There is an old wives' tale that I want to repeat a second time to complete this section.

**Myth:** *Cold air is unhealthy for little children and can cause respiratory infections and even pneumonia.* There is no truth to this one at all. The fact is that respiratory infections of all kinds are caused either by a virus or bacteria and are not related to cold weather. I have included this myth here again to encourage you to take your child outside *every chance you get, including cold days.* It is unfair to coop up an active young child during the winter months. The more opportunities she has to run and jump and climb, the stronger and healthier she will become.

SAFETY TIPS

**Choking.** All your baby's toys should be unbreakable and have no small parts or sharp edges. Keep your child away from chewing gum, popcorn, peanuts, and small balls. It is easy for a baby to choke.

**Burns and electric shocks.** Never leave your child unattended in the kitchen; it is a danger area. Teach her the meaning of hot. Always keep matches out of sight. While cooking, get into the habit of only using the back burners and of turning the pot handles to the wall. As part of your child-proofing, cover your electric outlets with safety plugs if you have not already done so. Place guards in front of wall heaters, fireplaces, and steam radiators. Be especially careful with electric cords that are attached to coffee pots and the like. This is a common cause of severe burns at this age.

**Poisons.** Since everything goes into the mouth, poisoning is quite common during this period. It is important to realize that babies do not seem to worry about the odors of various substances. The smell, no matter how unpleasant it might be to you, does not act as a deterrent to a child. Here are some suggestions about dealing with poisonous substances in your home:

1. As I suggested in the previous chapter, keep a one-ounce bottle of syrup of ipecac in your medicine cabinet. Check with your doctor as to the dosage to be used if your child accidentally swallows a poisonous substance. Syrup of ipecac induces vomiting.
2. Always keep products in their original containers. Never put inedible products into food or beverage containers.
3. Always read the label carefully before using any product.
4. Since your child is a great imitator, get into the habit of not taking any medicine when she is around.
5. Get rid of any oil of wintergreen you might have in the house. This is a deadly poison and of no real therapeutic value.

   We had a recent case of oil of wintergreen poisoning at the hospital with which I am affiliated. A two-year-old drank one teaspoon of it. That small amount is a lethal dose of salicylates, and we were fortunate that the baby survived.
6. Statistics have shown that the children who have ingested a poisonous substance one time are more likely to do it again. Therefore, if your child already has been involved with a poison, be especially alert and careful so that it *will not* happen again.
7. It is gratifying to report that the death rates from poisoning in the United States in the past ten years have decreased along with the appearance of regulated safety packaging on containers of aspirin, furniture polish, drain cleaners, prescriptions, and the like. Nevertheless, the 1976 mortality report from the National Center for Health Statistics showed that 105 children below five years of age died of accidental poisoning. Many small children are still able to open safety packages. Enough said on this subject.

## EMOTIONAL (SOCIAL) DEVELOPMENT

The question of toilet training is often raised at around this age. I have chosen to discuss it in the next chapter (Two to Three Years) because I believe that any serious attempts at training your child should not start much before the age of two. It is true, however, that some eighteen-month-olds are ready to be toilet trained. If you think that this may be the case with your child, you can read about my approach to this subject in the next chapter.

There are three important general areas related to the emotional development of your child that I want to discuss with you before giving my specific recommendations for helping her to achieve maximum emotional maturity. These are discipline, slowing down, and body talk.

### DISCIPLINE

Negative behavior and temper tantrums should be expected, and there is no sense in kidding you — they can be very difficult to manage. Some call this period of your child's life an early form, or better yet, a preview, of her adolescent rebellion period later on.

All of us surely agree that children must be taught to control their behavior on a day-to-day basis so that they can eventually learn to rely on themselves, rather than on adults, to decide what is right and what is wrong. However, there are large areas of disagreement in terms of how best to accomplish this. The word discipline comes from the word "disciple," meaning someone who follows the teachings of another. Discipline therefore should mean the learning experiences you give your child, and not simply punishment. Unfortunately, many parents as well as professionals equate discipline with punishment. When a child misbehaves, she often does so to show her independence, to learn a new skill (such as smashing dishes on the floor), or to express her feelings of frustration. From her point of view these are all sound and valid reasons for her negative behavior. I am not for a moment advocating that you should always approve of what she does. There will be times when you will have to act promptly in order to stop her from hurting herself or somebody else. But at least if you understand why she is acting up in this fashion, you will be in a better position to cope with it.

There are a number of techniques that can be used to help teach your child to change her behavior, to stop her destructive tendencies and temper tantrums, and to encourage self-control and self-discipline.

133

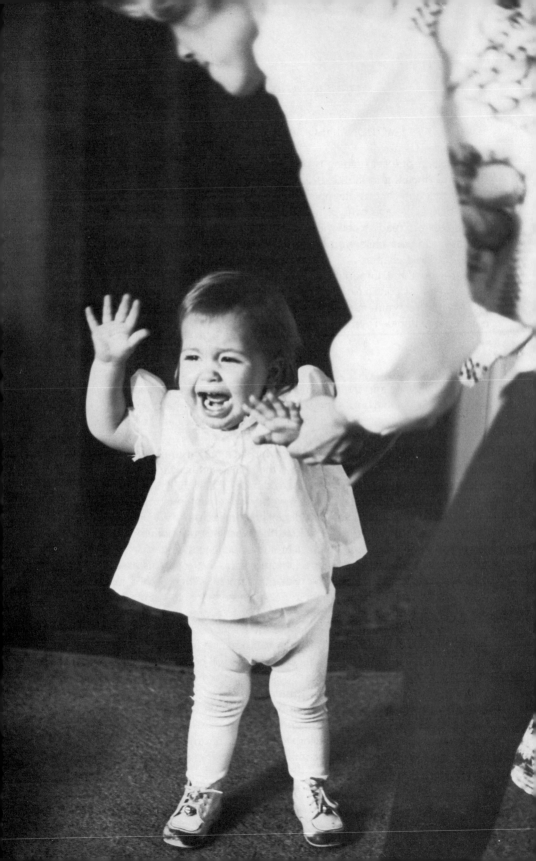

**Distract her.** This may not work too well at this age, but it is worth a try. Whenever possible, try to distract or redirect your child to another activity. For example, try playing some music, or sing a song together. As the old saying goes, "Music has charms to sooth a savage breast," and sometimes it also soothes a savage child.

**Separation.** One effective method of disciplining (teaching) your child when she misbehaves is to simply take her away from the place of trouble. For example, if she is in the park playing and suddenly decides to bite her friend, separate her from the situation and take her back home. Screaming and yelling at her is a waste of your time and doesn't teach her anything except how to scream and yell herself. She learns by example, and no other way.

**Explanation.** If you find it necessary to remove your child from an area or activity because of her misbehavior, try to explain to her why you are doing so. Establishing a rule or regulation and not explaining why you have done so will make it very difficult for your child to understand and adhere to the rules.

**Compromises.** You and your child will have many, many differences of opinion, and every once in a while it is helpful if you give in and let your child have her way. If you are having a dispute whose outcome is not particularly important, that is the time to compromise. To put it another way, allow your child to make some decisions on her own. Let her win some of the small arguments and you'll have a better chance of winning the big ones.

**Punishment.** There is a place for punishment in teaching discipline. Spanking or taking away privileges from your child should be reserved for important situations. Some examples of what I call important situations are when your little child decides to turn on the gas jets on the stove, or runs out into the street, or has a violent temper tantrum. If you punish her too often for every minor infraction of the rules, any type of punishment, including spanking, will lose its effectiveness. I would recommend that you save hitting or spanking for those few occasions when your child's behavior is totally unacceptable and for those times when your child tries to harm herself or somebody else.

Since West Point does not accept one-and-a-half or even two-year-olds, I would advise you not to treat your child as though she were in military school. There are times when you will have to put your foot down and take firm and definitive action. Save those occasions for the moments that really count, and look the other way when her mis-behavior is merely a little bit out of line.

## SLOWING DOWN

This is a subject that very few parents think about. If you find that you always seem to be in a hurry because you are so very busy, your little child may be getting the wrong message from you. She cannot as yet understand that you really have so much to do each day. She will start to think that she is just not important enough for you to spend much time with her. I realize that sometimes there just are not enough hours in the day to get everything done, but nonetheless you should try to slow down and spend more time holding and touching and talking to your child. Bathing, feeding, and dressing her on the run is not enough. Your child must be reassured of your love every single day, and this takes a certain amount of quiet time besides lots of good intentions.

## BODY TALK

Despite the fact that your child's usable vocabulary is growing during these six months, your baby will still do a lot of her "talking" with her body and through her behavior. Many of us do not pay enough atten-tion to this body talk because we assume that at this age, the child will communicate her needs to us verbally. Actually, without using any rec-ognizable words, your child still can give you many clues as to what she wants — by her expression, gestures, tone of voice, various moods, and actions. You can rest assured that she will get your attention one way or another. If you are not attuned to what she wants, she may smash her favorite toy in frustration or have a full-blown temper tantrum. The point I am trying to make is that you should "listen" to your child's body talk and respond appropriately. If she is unable to make her wishes known to you over and over again because she does not yet have the verbal competence to do so and you cannot understand her body language, she will become discouraged and withdrawn or negative and hostile.

## SPECIFIC RECOMMENDATIONS

The following are my specific suggestions for helping your child's emo-tional development.

**Make-believe games.** During these six months many babies start make-believe play, although some don't do very much of this until after their second birthday. Your child now develops a better sense of reality and a real sense of "self." Because of this, imaginative play is very useful in helping her deal with her feelings. For example, she will now be able to scold or yell at her doll or, if she feels like it, to kiss and cuddle the doll instead. She can play "mama" and she has a vehicle through which to express her feelings. Psychologists call this role playing. Of course, now she can also talk to her doll. Most of the time you won't be able to understand what she is saying to her doll, but as long as the doll understands, everything is fine. For these make-believe games, supply your child with a variety of dolls and stuffed animals. Also give her a toy telephone, which is not only a great prop for make-believe conversations, but also helps build up her language skills. The Fisher-Price Family Castle is a fine toy for make-believe games. It has a trap door, secret rooms, horses, dolls of a royal family, and furniture. It can last for a long time and can continue to be used as your child grows older. Dump trucks, toy carriages, and toy fire engines are also very much appreciated by all young children, as are empty boxes of all shapes and sizes.

It will not be difficult for you to improvise all sorts of make-believe games, and I can assure you that your child will enjoy all of them. For example, take one of her crayons and teach her to imagine that it is not a crayon but a car, instead. Push the crayon around the floor and make the noise of a car. After awhile she will understand what you are doing and will join the fun. She may take another crayon and use it as a car herself or she may go to her toy chest and bring out a real toy car instead.

By giving her the tools to deal more easily with her own feelings, you will help to build up her emotional stability and feelings of self-worth, and these feelings will remain with her as she grows and matures.

About this age nightmares may begin. With the start of symbolic-level thinking (to be discussed in the section on mental development), nightmares occur. This is an example of distorted reality. I have been called a number of times by parents and told about nightmares occurring soon after one traumatic experience or another. I was even blamed for one little boy's nightmare because it took place the very night after I had sutured a laceration on his head that was associated with much screaming and yelling.

**Chores.** Although I discussed chores in the physical development section of this chapter, I am including them here too because household chores are also an effective way to teach your child about cooperation, they also help to make her feel that she is a real part of the family. The sooner she learns about cooperation and about being part of the family, the better, in terms of what kind of person she will turn out to be.

**Promises and threats.** With negativism, stubbornness, and selfishness all integral parts of your child's behavior at this age, it will be very easy for you to make idle threats or idle promises that you will not be able or want to keep. I remember one mother who was so upset with her twenty-month-old son's behavior that she threatened *never* to allow Michael to visit his friend again if he did not immediately stop tearing up his books. Never is a little too long. My advice is never to make a promise or a threat unless you are prepared to stick to your word.

A recent study sponsored by the National Institute of Mental Health in Washington concluded that parents who kept their promises had children who grew up to be trusting parents themselves. Parents who are careless about or unable to keep their promises or who promise their children anything to keep them quiet or to change their behavior do irreparable harm. Parents of this type may cause their children to develop deep suspicions of others and a pessimistic approach to life. If your child cannot believe what you tell her, how can you expect her ever to believe what anybody else tells her?

**Music.** Most eighteen- to twenty-four-month-olds can learn to use a push-in type of record player after they've been given a few demonstrations. Such a record player will allow your child to decide for herself when to play music. Little children should be encouraged to dance and move rhythmically in time to music since this is a splendid way for them to learn to become more attuned to their bodies. In the next chapter (Two to Three Years) I will be discussing the concept of positive body image and what you can do to help your child learn to love her own body. For now, let me say that learning to dance is one way of helping to achieve a good feeling about one's own body. I believe that getting your child a record player all her own at this time is a very wise decision.

Playing rhythm instruments (as mentioned in the previous chapter) remains a fine activity for your child. A house that is full of music (even if the music may not exactly be to your own taste) is a happier place for your child.

**Play-doh.** This is helpful for creative and dramatic play. Play-doh is less messy than regular clay and is reusable if it is kept in a closed, airtight container when not in use. Some parents complain about the way it smells, but children don't seem to mind the odor. Your child can mold it into various shapes and forms and will take great pride in her artwork.

*"Let-go" time.* Your little child now requires more time for herself. She will be initiating her own activities and playing on her own, and you should encourage her. By allowing her this independence, you will be better preparing her to face future activities outside the home, such as at a day-care center or nursery school. We call the time your child spends by herself "let-go" time. It is hard for some parents to believe or accept the fact that their children simply don't need them all the time anymore. Your eighteen- to twenty-four-month-old must be given the opportunity to fend for herself part of each day, so don't be afraid to let go.

An example of let-go time is when you are home doing your chores in one room or area of the house while your baby is playing by herself in another room. Every once in a while she will come to you to make sure that you are still around and perhaps to show you what she is doing, and then she will go back to her own activity. This is fine for her independence and feelings of self-worth. Such an arrangement helps her become her own person. It is important that you (or the primary caretaker) be where she can find you. If you let go too fast or too far — such as, for example, suddenly disappearing entirely from the scene without telling her — your child will become very frightened and insecure. If you do this too often, the chances are that she will start hanging onto your apron strings all day long because she will always be afraid that you will desert her again.

*Self-esteem.* Because I have repeated it so often, you probably are getting the idea that I believe very strongly that building up your child's self-esteem and self-image is one of the most important contributions you can ever make to her future emotional well-being and success in school and beyond. You are right; that is exactly what I believe. Helping to give your little child a positive sense of self-worth is truly one of the major obligations and duties of being a positive parent. If you continuously "put her down," criticize, and correct her, and make her feel inadequate and stupid (however well-intentioned your motives may be), you will cause her to become unsure of herself and less confident in her own abilities. This will result in her losing interest and initiative in learning, simply because she will be afraid of failing again. She will stop trying as hard. This surely will be reflected in her later school and work performance. Always encourage rather than discourage your child. Neither expect nor demand perfection. Setting unrealistic goals is the surest and fastest way to destroy your child's self-confidence.

**Curiosity.** Continue to encourage your child's curiosity and her adventurous spirit. If she happens to fail in a task, don't reprimand her. Rather, tell her that it is perfectly all right. Show her that you're happy she tried, and don't worry about whether or not she is successful. It is only by trying that she will eventually learn, and if she is secure in the knowledge that you are not judging her each time, she will remain enthusiastic and anxious to expand her learning experiences. The chances are that how she thinks about herself now will probably be how she thinks of herself later on, when she starts school. With her curiosity and optimism intact, she is much more likely to be successful.

To end this section, I would like to explode another old wives' tale.

**Myth:** *Thumb sucking at this age is a sure sign of emotional trouble.* Not true at all. The majority of children who are still sucking their thumbs between eighteen and twenty-four months of age are not at all emotionally disturbed. They just enjoy sucking their thumbs. I might add that there is another myth about thumb sucking — that it will ruin the child's permanent teeth alignment. Again, not true. It is true that with vigorous thumb sucking the baby teeth may be pushed out of line, but if the thumb sucking stops before age four, it is very unlikely that the permanent teeth will be affected.

### MENTAL (INTELLECTUAL) DEVELOPMENT

I want to start this section with a warning. Don't try to push your little child too hard or too fast. With her remarkable advances in real thinking, it will be very easy for you to inadvertently overburden her learning capacity during these six months. Too much stimulation has been shown to be just as detrimental to optimum mental development as too little stimulation. It has been proven that too much practice will make a child's response so automatic that an appropriate response will be more difficult to elicit when she is faced with a new learning situation. For example, if your child is given the same puzzle to solve over and over again and then finally is presented with a new puzzle, she will automatically respond to it in the same way she responded to the old one. This is called stereotyping, and it can result in developmental delays at any stage of concept development.

Another danger of overburdening is related to an overenriched environment, one that offers your child more than she can cope with. Children enjoy problem solving, but problems that are beyond their capabilities turn them off completely. If a child is faced with many problems that she is not ready to solve, she will withdraw and retreat and lose interest in solving any problems. What I mean is that it is just as bad to expect too much from your child as it is to not challenge her mind at all. The trick is to try to make sure that what you offer her neither bores nor frustrates her but rather provides her with the environment that will stimulate her so that she can develop her intellectual capacities and competencies to their fullest.

Your child's mind now starts to function on a symbolic level. Your child is capable of storing and remembering images and ideas in her brain. An excellent example that explains symbolic thinking is presented in *Help Your Baby Learn,* by Stephen Lehane. He describes an eighteen-month-old girl of two blind parents who was trying to avoid being found by her father. This child wore bells on her shoes so that her blind parents could more easily locate where she was. This girl was observed to shuffle along slowly and gingerly step backwards because she realized that this type of movement would silence the ringing of the bells. She understood that she was actually fooling her father and held her hands up to her face, trying to control her giggling and laughing because she also understood that her noises would have betrayed her location. At one and a half years of age she not only had figured out the principle of not making noise with the bells and with her laughter, but she also was already able to manipulate and fool her parents. This very young lady was able to solve a most complicated and complex problem.

Your child will now begin to understand the concept of alternatives and options. This is the start of real thinking ability, of "thoughtfulness." She will be able to understand explanations and will have a pretty clear understanding of reality. What all this means is that the eighteen- to twenty-four-month-old starts figuring things out all by herself, which is a remarkable and exciting advance in her mental competency. Her problem-solving ability becomes more sophisticated. For example, she learns to use a stick to push a ball off a high shelf when she can't reach it with her hands. Abstract thinking also becomes part of her intellectual armamentarium. Whereas previously she understood that her block was the only block there was, now she learns the *concept* of a block. In other words, she now realizes that there are all sorts of different-sized, different-shaped, and different-colored blocks with one common denominator: the characteristics of a block. This holds true for bottles, for dishes, for balls, and other objects.

The eighteen- to twenty-four-month-old also usually learns to master two additional complicated and difficult concepts, conservation and numbers.

## CONSERVATION

The concept of conservation means that a child understands that an object is the same even though it actually looks different when its shape is changed. It also means that the child realizes that the weight of an object is unrelated to any change in its shape. Before this, a child believes that all objects are the same weight, and that the larger or longer the object, the heavier it is. When you think about it, the ability to make this transition in perception is indeed a remarkable advance in a child's intellectual ability.

## NUMBERS

It may be hard for you to believe that a child between eighteen and twenty-four months of age can actually *count* even though she has no understanding of numbers. *A Primer of Infant Development* by T.G.R. Bower describes an interesting experiment proving this to be true. A number of children around eighteen months of age were given a series of two groups of pieces of candy from which they were asked to select the group containing more pieces of candy.

*Illustrations*

| | |
|:---:|:---:|
| 0 0 0 0 0 | 0 0 0 |
| 0    0    0 | 0 0 0 0 0 |
| Equal length, | Different length, |
| different density | equal density |
| 0  0  0  0  0 | 0    0    0 |
| 0    0    0 | 0  0  0  0  0 |
| Different length, | Different length, |
| different density | different density |

Any way the two groups were presented, most of these little children were able to select the group that contained more pieces of candy. Whether or not you agree that this is actually counting, it is in fact a real beginning of mathematical reasoning.

## VERBAL COMPETENCE

As I mentioned at the beginning of this chapter, you will now witness great strides forward in verbal competence. By age two your child probably will have a working vocabulary of twenty words or more and also will be able to say a few simple two-word phrases. She will start to ask for things with words and may start using the word "me." Instead of using her own name she will begin to say "me want" instead. Although the results are in a sense obvious, you might be interested in a recent anthropological study conducted at Stanford University by Dr. Chevalier-Skolnikoff which involved infant apes and infant humans during the first two years of life. The results demonstrated an almost identical behavior pattern month by month in both groups, with one essential difference. The infant apes' vocalization process stopped at an early age, and this is considered the vital factor in the subsequent maturation of both species. Apes never coo or babble and never acquire more sophisticated modes of vocalization. The important point to remember is that speech and language appear to be the principal mode of future learning and socialization. Put another way, language is what separates humans from the rest of the animal kingdom. Therefore, helping your child acquire verbal competence is most important for her future intellectual accomplishments.

Before giving you my specific recommendations to help your child reach her maximum intellectual potential, allow me to put to rest another widely held misconception that relates to mental development.

**Myth:** *A fever convulsion causes brain damage.* Not true. The type of convulsion that is caused by only high fever (most of which occurs between one to two years of age) does not result in brain damage. Such a seizure can be very frightening, but if handled properly, is easily managed. I would suggest that you discuss this subject with your child's physician so that you know what to do if and when it happens.

## SPECIFIC RECOMMENDATIONS

Below are some specific recommendations about activities, and equipment (your child will invent many other activities on her own, and should be encouraged to do so).

**Puzzles.** The more, the merrier. Your child is getting better at solving puzzles all the time. She will be able to learn to put together simple jigsaw puzzles. You can make your own with construction paper or cardboard. All you have to do is cut out various shapes and show her what to do. This type of puzzle will help her learn about size, position, and shape. You can also purchase wooden or plastic puzzles, always making sure they are simple, with just a few familiar objects. Modular sets to fit together are also useful for building and for learning about design and these also increase her manual dexterity.

**Guessing games.** Among these, a favorite is a takeoff on the well-known "shell game" used by gamblers to fleece unsuspecting and greedy participants. All you need are three different-sized cans and a toy small enough to fit under each of the cans. Place the toy under one of them and show your baby what you have done. Next, move the cans around and then ask her to tell you where the toy is. If she guesses right, you both should be very happy. If she makes a mistake, don't get upset, but say, "No, it is not there. Try again." In a relatively short period of time she should be able to get the hang of it, and then it's time to move on to a more difficult version. This time, actually hide the toy under one of the cans, always remembering to hide it under the largest one, and ask her to find it. It will take varying amounts of time, but sooner or later she will realize what you are doing and will be able to pick out the correct (largest) can. If you stop to think about it, this is quite an accomplishment. She has been able to reason and figure out that the toy is always hidden under the largest can. Another variation is to turn things around and ask her to to hide the toy and have you guess. Colored cans or cans with different labels can be used as well. Remember always to hide the toy in a consistent manner so that the game does not become strictly one of guessing.

Never make things too difficult for your child, and above all, don't tease or criticize her when she makes a mistake. There are endless variations you can devise. This kind of activity teaches your child about space relations, size, shape, and location, and promotes reasoning and problem solving ability. It is so effective because it is challenging, lots of fun, and never boring.

**Going places.** I have said it before and I will say it again now: it is important to take your child out of the house as often as possible — to the park, zoo, museum, and airport. Trips in the automobile, to children's theaters, and to restaurants should be planned whenever possible. Your child will enjoy these expeditions and will have the opportunity to absorb much valuable information, provided you take the time to talk to her and explain exactly what she is seeing and doing. Since children at this age understand up to several hundred different words and phrases, they are more than ready to listen and respond to what you have to say.

**Anatomy.** It is quite important for your child to learn about the various parts of her body and their functions. Little children are fascinated with their bodies and are anxious to learn all they can. Point and ask, touch and ask: "Where is your mouth? Your vagina? Where are your eyes?" Teach her what each part of her body does. For example, ears are for hearing, eyes for seeing and mouths for opening and chewing. Cover your child's eyes and then say, "Now you can't see." I once was witness to an amazing show of knowledge in anatomy put on by a mother and her twenty-one-month-old girl. That child not only knew the obvious parts of her body but also could point, without making a single mistake, to her clavicle, sternum, knee, wrist, and, as a matter of fact, to just about every single part of her little body. I did not ask, but I am pretty sure that Mrs. P. was preparing her daughter for early entry into medical school!

**Functions of objects.** There is no reason to dwell on this in great detail. It is obvious that teaching your child the functions of the various objects she sees is the cornerstone of her learning processes. If you see an airplane, make the appropriate sound effects and say that the airplane flies. Do the same with a dog or a fire engine or anything else. If you happen to be outside with your child and you see an automobile moving, watch it together and imitate its sound. When you're back home take out her toy automobile and repeat the process. Use your child's familiar toys and objects and show her how they work. For example, demonstrate that the doll can sit, stand, or lie down and her truck can move and make sounds.

**Blocks.** These are ideal for creative play. Your child will be able to arrange blocks in groups (sorting them) according to their size, shape, and color, and will build block towers with considerable skill and imagination. As an example of what you can do, take two red blocks and two green blocks and show her the difference in color. Then take one of the red blocks and ask her to give you the other red block. Although she will not be able to name the actual color, she can learn about different colors at this age. Similarly, you can ask for blocks of the same size or for the little block, and on and on.

The Tupperware toy, a ball made up of shaped, plastic blocks that can be pulled out by tugging on various handles is a good example of a block toy. Your child will pull it apart and can be taught with your help to put it back together again. This is an excellent sorting game. After she has learned to handle it, she can play alone with it for relatively long periods of time.

**Crayons, pencils, and paper.** Your baby now is a great scribbler, and with practice can learn to imitate a pretty straight line and sometimes can even make a reasonable attempt at imitating a circle. All this is excellent preparation for her school work later on. Don't expect too much. Remember, penmanship does not count yet.

**Mechanical skills.** It has been my experience that many parents do not pay enough attention to this area of development at this time. Your child now has the ability and ambition to learn all sorts of mechanical skills. She can be taught to turn on television sets, radios, and light switches. She can learn to put coins into laundromat machines and parking meters and should be taught to buckle her own seat belt. These are all useful skills and improve her manual dexterity as well as giving her feelings of participation. Handling a simple record player with an on-and-off-switch mechanism and nonbreakable records is well within the mechanical capabilities of most eighteen- to twenty-four-month-olds. Pressing elevator buttons is something you can allow your youngster to do, and which will immediately reward her. The elevator will move because of her skill in button pushing, and she will know it. Of course, unless she is pretty tall for her age, it will be necessary for you to lift her to the level of the elevator buttons. I remember driving across the Triboro Bridge when our son was about two years old and I thought that he was ready to throw the quarter (the tolls were much cheaper in those days) into the basket at the toll booth. He gave it a good try but missed badly. We had sense enough not to criticize him for his wild pitch. He was more successful in throwing the quarter into the basket six months later and he's had a perfect record ever since.

**Memory.** Since your child's memory is improving so dramatically, you should give her every opportunity to develop it. For example, read her a story; then, a couple of hours later, ask her a question about the story, such as, "How did the dog bark?" Children at this age are excellent imitators and mimics of things they have seen or heard. Don't expect your child to remember the details of a story that you may have read to her three days earlier — although I must admit, some of these little chil-

dren have memories like steel traps and never seem to forget anything. Memory, like everything else, varies from child to child, so I would advise you not to compare your child's memory with that of the child next door.

**Hide and seek.** Since now your child can actually picture objects and locations in her head, hide-and-seek games can be played on a more sophisticated level. She will be able to look for missing or hidden toys and will not give up as easily as before. These hide-and-seek games are best played with other children. Some psychologists believe that understanding the concept that something hidden or missing can be found, makes it easier for your child to accept your leaving her on occasion. This is because she will not worry so much that you won't ever come back. I honestly do not know whether or not this is true. I do know that hide-and-seek games give little children a great deal of pleasure, and besides, they are good learning experiences.

**Television.** I have already made my position clear about television at this age, but now I want to hedge a little. Many parents tell me that their eighteen- to twenty-four-month-olds do seem to enjoy watching short segments of selected children's programs such as "Sesame Street" and "Captain Kangaroo." An occasional viewing of one of these programs may be a good listening and learning experience for some children at this age, and you can try some of the activities performed on these programs with your youngster. However, basically I still believe that most children get very little out of television-watching until they are past two years of age.

**Laughter.** Why am I including laughter in the section on mental rather than emotional development? It really belongs in both, but I have chosen to put it here to emphasize the importance of laughter in terms of intellectual achievement. A recent three-year study was conducted by Dr. Abner Ziz, an Israeli psychologist. He concluded that people retain better what they are taught when the teacher uses humor. Laughter helps learning at any age. It is a very good idea to always keep this in mind.

## LANGUAGE

We have already discussed the crucial importance of language and what you can expect from your child at this age. To repeat, by two years of age many children have a vocabulary of twenty words, and at times up to fifty words, and understand up to several hundred different words and phrases.

**Talking.** The key to achieving verbal competence is for you to talk to your child and also to listen to what she says without interrupting her. If you are not certain what she has said, don't ignore it; rather, ask her to repeat it. A language characteristic of this age is rapid jabbering, called jargon. The avalanche of words that pour out of a child's mouth are full of expression that has no meaning for you. Some call this jabbering "verbal diarrhea," but I don't particularly like that expression because it has the connotation of a put down. Jargon is important and you should not be upset or tell your child to slow down her talking. Jargon is a prelude to the next stage, understandable language, and all children have to go through it.

Don't criticize your child's words but rather repeat the word or words correctly, and don't get into the habit of using baby talk. You should ask her for various objects; for example, say, "Show me the red block." Talk to her about such characteristics of objects as top and bottom, heavy or light, wet or dry, hot or cold, and the like. This is the way you can best give your child the words which she will then be able to use to articulate her ideas and thoughts. This is what verbal competence is all about.

**Reading.** There are many excellent story books you can read to your child. Don't be surprised if she prefers to hear the same story over and over again. There is no question that verbal competence is difficult to achieve without a good deal of reading. And don't forget to continue the bedtime reading ritual.

Books with large pictures are required at this age. Point to a picture and explain what it is and what it does or have her point to a picture and then tell her all about it. One of the best ways to insure that your child will do well in school later on is to help her develop language skills now.

In order to keep this whole discussion of language development in proper perspective, I'd like to quote what the mother of a fine twenty-two-month-old boy told me recently in my office. "John's working vocabulary is a grand total of three words but he understands pretty much everything that is spoken to him." About his sparse vocabulary, she had this to say: "When he's ready, he's ready." I could not agree more with what his most intelligent mother said. There is just so much you can do to help your child talk, and no more. When she's ready, the words will come.

Happy second birthday!

# CHAPTER VII

# Two to
# Three Years

**INTRODUCTION**

The two- to three-year-old will begin to construct a new world on the level of verbalization and representation. With his rapidly advancing language skills and his growing ability to think on a symbolic level, he is in a much stronger position to learn about and master more and more of the world around him. Because children of this age can talk and reason and understand, many parents make the serious mistake of pushing them too hard by trying to teach them more than they can handle. The trick is to allow and encourage your child to do as many tasks as he is able without trying to rush him too fast into the adult world. You should always keep in mind that many of the two- to three-year-olds' mental processes are quite immature yet, and he continues to make many er-

rors in his reasoning. For example, a child at this age still believes that anything that moves is alive. Logical reasoning takes many years to master, so it is important that you not expect too much from your child at this age and not overburden him with problems that he is not yet capable of solving.

As I discussed in the previous chapter, a balanced approach is the best one to take. Too much pressure on your baby to learn how to speak or to solve problems will not only slow down his intellectual progress but will also surely lead to difficulties in his emotional development. As Dr. Burton White writes in *The First Three Years of Life*, " . . . intellectual superiority is very frequently obtained at the expense of progress in other areas of equal or even greater importance."

One of the cornerstones of intellectual achievement is the child's ability to master symbolic thinking. In *Piaget's Theory of Intellectual Development*, by Herbert Ginsburg and Sylvia Opper, the definition of symbolic thinking is given as the ability to make a mental symbol, an object, or a word represent something else that is not present at that time. These authors give as an example of symbolic thinking a two- to three-year-old who can make a mental symbol or picture of a bicycle or the word "bicycle" or a small schematic toy of a bicycle to stand for the real bicycle when it is not in immediate view. This advanced thinking ability allows the child to operate on new and expanded levels. He no longer is restricted to act only upon objects he can see because he now can use a mental picture to remember what he has learned in the past. Because he can now form a mental picture of a bicycle, he is in a position to remember his previous experiences with bicycles.

Piaget believes that symbolic play (make-believe play) is essential for your child's emotional stability and for his ability to adjust to reality. Children between two and three years of age spend a good deal of their time in symbolic play. You should encourage this type of play since your child can use make-believe play to act out the conflicts of his real life in such a way as to make sure he comes out the winner. In real life he often comes out the loser because there are many things he wants that he cannot get and many thoughts he wants to express that he is not yet capable of expressing.

There is one word that best describes the basic characteristic of the two- to three-year-old, and that word is egocentric. By egocentric we mean that the child sees and understands the world entirely and exclusively from his own point of view. I recall a conversation with the mother of a two-and-a-half-year-old who could not understand why Walter was so selfish. "Why can't he understand that I accidentally hit him on the side of his head while I was reaching for one of his toys?" I explained to her that the concept of an "accident" is beyond a two-and-a-half-year-old's comprehension. All little Walter knew was that he was hit on the side of his head by his mother and this certainly made him extremely angry.

Unfortunately, by the time they reach age two, some children are already "spoiled" and difficult to live with. These youngsters are often angry and hostile and not very lovable much of the time. I will be discussing the subject of anger in some detail in the section on emotional development in this chapter. Although some of your child's personality traits may already be fairly well-established, you can still do much to mold the positive attributes of his personality and to minimize his negative traits. The good news about two- to three-year-olds is that many become less negative than they were at eighteen to twenty-four months of age; if this is the case in your house, be grateful. You can take some of the credit, but don't rest on your laurels.

During this year, children are better able to play alongside other children, and this type of parallel play should be encouraged. This will better prepare them for the next step, which is cooperative play. However, do not expect your child at this age to engage in active play with other children (cooperative play). That will not really start until he is over three years old, a good age to enter nursery school. Since most children of this age enjoy playing by themselves, at times for relatively long periods, some parents assume that they will also be able to play peacefully and contentedly with and alongside another child or two. This is a false assumption. If these little children are, in fact, allowed to play together in an unsupervised situation, chaos and destruction are sure to follow. Take my advice when I tell you that at this stage, play periods involving your child and other children should always be supervised.

By and large these twelve months are a happy and exciting time for your child. Even though he is egocentric and thinks only about himself and is interested in his own instant gratification and so is often frustrated, he is very resilient and bounces right back if given half a chance. At this age he is physically able to run, jump and climb, he can now verbalize many of his needs, and he learns to carry on a two-way conversation. He remains full of energy and enthusiasm. He still takes great pride in his personal accomplishments, and you must continue to praise him for his efforts. This raises an interesting question related to the building up of his self-esteem. Some parents are so caught up with this part of their child's emotional development that they don't take into consideration what the child has actually accomplished. There is a limit to how much you should praise your child. It is foolish and counterproductive to make a big fuss over every trivial deed. Both you and your child will know when he really does something worthwhile, and those are the times to tell and show him how proud you are of his success. I am not suggesting that you should withhold reacting positively to his accomplishments, but rather that you be somewhat selective when praising him. This approach will motivate him to do his very best and not be content just to coast along on his previous achievements. It will also better prepare him to compete later on in school, where there is no such thing as unrealistic praise.

You will notice that your child is now even more attuned and sensitive to everything that is going on around him. He does not miss a thing. Mr. and Mrs. B., a devoted and loving couple, were the proud parents of three-year-old Christopher. Mrs. B. told me about the time her husband came home from work one day so tired and harassed that he was not in any mood to kiss her "hello," something he did every single night. Christopher picked right up on this and ran to his father, quite upset, and said, "Daddy no kiss Mommy." Incidentally, I believe that it is important for parents to show affection toward each other in front of their children. In my experience, many parents often don't. It is almost as if they are trying to hide overt affectionate advances when their children are around. I also think it is important to show kindness and consideration and thoughtfulness to each other as well as to the child. It is axiomatic that children learn by example: everything you do rubs off on your child.

I want to discuss with you now two words that I have not used up to this point; namely, *optimism* and *courage*. I have been struck by the fact that most of the really successful people (both children and adults) I have met through the years have had more than their fair share of these two qualities. I am referring to bank presidents, heads of corporations, leading lawyers and physicians, professors, honor students, class presidents, and others who might be characterized as leaders. The majority are both optimistic and courageous in their approach to life. I have discussed this with many educators, and they agree with me that this has also been their observation. The logical conclusion to be drawn from this is that a high level of achievement is more likely to occur when one has these two basic personality traits. Optimism and courage develop in large measure out of a positive self-image and self-esteem, and pessimism and timidity are the inevitable results of a lack of self-confidence. The courage to take risks and not to dwell upon and worry about honest mistakes, but rather to learn from them and push on optimistically from there, is the hallmark of the truly successful, productive person. You, as a parent, will play a large role in determining whether your child will grow up with enough self-confidence to be in a position to achieve the very best that is in him. Your child must be given the freedom and opportunity to experiment and make mistakes without feeling guilty. Although I have not previously used the actual words, I have nevertheless focused on giving you the information and recommendations to help you help your child become a courageous and optimistic human being. The rest of this chapter will continue to be devoted to the same purpose.

## 2–3 Years

### GROWTH AND DEVELOPMENT
#### *Physical (Motor)*

1. Walks up and down stairs without difficulty.
2. Climbs, runs, and jumps with agility and precision.
3. Kicks a ball and throws it with some accuracy.
4. Good hand/eye coordination.
5. Enjoys playing with and manipulating small objects.
6. Learns to ride a tricycle.
7. Handles crayon and pencil well.
8. Scribbles and can copy lines and circles.
9. Can feed himself without much difficulty.
10. Can carry heavy objects and push and pull with strength.

*Note:* These charts are based on average *ranges* of growth and development; many normal children perform and achieve either sooner or later than indicated.

## 2–3 Years

### GROWTH AND DEVELOPMENT
#### *Emotional (Social)*

1. Increased attention span.
2. Behavior usually less negative and stubborn.

3. Independent; enjoys doing things for himself.
4. Great involvement in fantasy or make-believe play.
5. Egocentric: sees and understands things completely from his own point of view.
6. Enjoys playing alongside other children (not ready for cooperative play).
7. Possessive of his belongings but still can be taught to share.
8. Spends more time playing away from primary caretaker.
9. Sensitive to the feelings of people around him.
10. More time spent in role playing.
11. Bowel toilet training usually accomplished.
12. Enjoys set routine and "rituals" such as bedtime stories.

*Note:* These charts are based on average *ranges* of growth and development; many normal children perform and achieve either sooner or later than indicated.

## 2 – 3 Years

### GROWTH AND DEVELOPMENT
*Mental (Intellectual)*

1. Working vocabulary increases from fifty up to several hundred words by age three.
2. Learns to speak short (three- to four-word) sentences that can be understood even by strangers.
3. Understands the concept of numbers (one to many).
4. Uses "I" instead of his name.
5. Can identify many different pictures and objects.
6. Answers to and tells you his first (and sometimes his last) name.
7. "Hungry" to learn words and meanings.
8. Matches some colors.
9. Can put on his own shoes but cannot yet tie his laces.
10. Follows complicated directions of two or three tasks, one after another.
11. Memory greatly improved.
12. Symbolic thinking, reasoning, and thoughtfulness more advanced.
13. Problem solving improved; enjoys simple puzzles.
14. Can build block towers and forts.

*Note:* These charts are based on average *ranges* of growth and development; many normal children perform and achieve either sooner or later than indicated.

## PHYSICAL (MOTOR) DEVELOPMENT

With the physical well-being of your child in mind, I would like to briefly call your attention to two areas that should be reviewed and dealt with at this time: his immunization status and the examination of his eyes.

### IMMUNIZATIONS

In the three- to six-month chapter I discussed with you the importance of making certain that your child receive all the immunizations due him and that the primary series of these immunizations should be completed by the time he is two years old. Now is the appropriate time to check your records to see if in fact this is the case with your child. He should have received his primary series of Sabin oral polio drinks and a polio booster, three primary DPT shots (diphtheria, pertussis [whooping cough], and tetanus), and a DPT booster. He also should have already received an immunization against measles, rubella (German measles), and mumps, either in combination or separately. If you find that he is missing any of these protective shots, notify his doctor and arrange for an appointment to complete all the required immunizations.

### EYE EXAMINATIONS

Even if there is no obvious problem with your child's eyes such as strabismus (crossed eyes), it is good medical practice for him to have a careful eye examination no later than age three, either by the child's own physician or by an ophthalmologist or an optometrist. There is an eye condition called amblyopia (lazy-eye) that can cause a decrease or even loss of vision in the affected eye if not diagnosed in time. Amblyopia refers to the failure in development of binocular (two-eye) vision, and this results in the child not using one of his eyes to see. If lazy-eye is allowed to progress and continues for too long a period of time without proper treatment, there is partial or complete loss of vision in the eye that is not being used. The younger the child when the correct diagnosis is made, the better the chance of successful treatment. If caught early enough, treatment is relatively easy and effective. Unfortunately, in many children the problem is not suspected or picked up until they start school and have difficulty reading the blackboard. At that time it is usually too late to completely correct the visual defect. It is estimated that four out of one hundred preschool children suffer from amblyopia;

as you can see, this is not an uncommon problem. You can suspect lazy-eye if your child rubs his eyes excessively or shuts or covers one eye to see or tilts his head to one side or blinks frequently. If you notice any of these symptoms it is essential that you notify the child's doctor immediately. Even if he has no noticeable symptoms, he should have a careful eye examination by three years of age at the latest.

## NUTRITION

By this time your child should be accustomed to feeding himself regular table foods. The diet, it is hoped, has variety, is well-balanced and nutritious, and includes plenty of fruits and vegetables with a minimum of extra salt and sugar. We have already discussed between-meal snacks in the previous chapter. It will now become even more difficult for you to withhold or eliminate junk foods from your child's diet. During this year your child will probably be visiting the homes of other small children, and it is likely that some of their parents are already in the habit of stuffing their youngsters with these virtually nonnutritious, sugar-laden foods. If this is the case, I can assure you that it will not take very long for your child to acquire a strong preference for these sweet or salty junk foods. In addition, you will now be faced with strong competition from your television set regarding food choices, since many two- to three-year-olds become avid TV watchers (I will have more to say about television in the sections on exercises and mental development, which follow). The Group Action for Children's TV has established that the average television station on a Saturday morning shows eighteen commercials each hour, 65 percent of which are devoted to food. Of these food commercials, 60 percent are for sugar-laden foods. Your child will be continuously bombarded with this type of commercial, and as far as he is concerned, everything he hears on television is true. At this age he will start to tell you what foods he wants you to buy, and most of the time he will ask for those foods that he has seen and heard about on television. I had an interesting time talking about the subject of junk food television advertising when I appeared on the "Today" show discussing my first book, Growing Up Thin. I remember saying that I had yet to see a television commercial for carrots! That was a few years ago and I still have not seen one.

Although it won't be easy, it is important that you stand firm and not give in to pressures from your child to buy junk foods. In a discussion on this subject, Dr. Frederick Stare, the Harvard nutritionist, pointed out that the danger in eating too many junk foods is that they crowd out other nutritious foods. These junk foods will kill anyone's

appetite for wholesome, nourishing, and necessary foods. If you have the physical well-being of your child in mind, as I am sure you do, continue to "fat-proof" your house and avoid purchasing large quantities of junk foods. If they are readily available to your child each day, this is the real danger.

When he is between two and three years of age, the improved lines of verbal communication between you and your child can easily lead to many faulty feeding practices. It has been my experience that many parents will now use various foods as rewards for good behavior. "If you finish your string beans, you can have dessert." All this approach does is teach your child that the dessert is the most important part of the meal. This certainly doesn't make any sense. "If you stop throwing your toys all over the room, Mommy will give you a piece of candy." Yet another favorite line is, "If you really love mommy, you will finish all your spinach." The attitudes expressed here are all wrong. A child should not eat to please his parents, nor should he eat in order to receive a reward. The only reasons he should eat are to satisfy his hunger and supply his body with the proper nutrients for optimum growth and development.

In my practice I place every child who is two years of age or older, thin or fat, on what I call a "prudent" diet. By and large this is the same diet that adults with heart disease or high blood pressure are put on in order to slow down the development of atherosclerosis or hardening of the arteries. I want to make it clear that this is my personal recommendation and is still a somewhat controversial area. Therefore, before following these suggestions, I would recommend that you discuss them with your child's physician. My reasons for suggesting such a diet are simple and, in my opinion, quite sensible. Although this type of diet in young children has not as yet been proven to slow down the rate of hardening of the arteries, it may very well do so. Such a diet works for adults, so it makes good sense to me that it will work the same way in children — and if so, why not use it? If there is a family history of early heart disease on either side of the family, this is all the more reason to use the prudent diet. There is no question that the diet is healthy, well-balanced, and relatively low in calories, besides being low in cholesterol and saturated fats. There certainly is no harm in putting every child on such a diet. Finally, if a child grows up accustomed to eating this way, it is much more likely that he will continue to eat the same way as an adult. At that time there is little question that it will help protect him against the early onset of coronary heart disease and high blood pressure. There is everything to gain and nothing to lose with such a diet, which is why I recommend it for all children two years of age and older.

Dr. Ronald Lauer, Professor of Pediatrics at the University of Iowa School of Medicine, agrees with this approach. Dr. Lauer was a guest speaker for the Leo M. Taren Memorial Lecture at the New York University School of Medicine during May, 1980. Based on his research in "tracking" the various heart disease risk factors in children, and the epidemiologic evidence to date, he believes that it makes intuitive good sense to put all children beyond infancy on a "prudent" diet.

The following are the main features of the diet:

**Eggs.** Egg yolk is extremely high in cholesterol (one of the risk factors in heart disease), so in order to keep down total cholesterol intake, the number of eggs eaten should be restricted to a maximum of three or four per week.

**Skim milk.** Skim milk is just as healthy as regular milk and has less fat and fewer calories. I recommend skim milk for all children at this age, not only the fat ones.

**Meats and fish.** Red meats (pork and beef), which are high in saturated fats, and organ meats (liver, brain, kidney, sweetbreads) are all high in cholesterol and should not be eaten more than two to three times per week. Saturated fats are another risk factor in heart disease and their total consumption should be reduced. Instead of red meat, I would suggest that you eat more veal, poultry, and fish. I suggest not serving shrimp too often since it is also extremely high in cholesterol.

**Sugars.** Cut down on the intake of refined and processed sugars. This can readily be accomplished by keeping junk foods out of the house. I am referring to cake, candy, soda, and cookies. I am not advocating that these foods be totally eliminated. I am suggesting that they be kept down to a minimum and served only on special occasions.

**Salt.** It is not necessary to add salt to foods since there is plenty of natural salt already there. One accepted method of lowering high blood pressure is to reduce salt intake, so why risk giving excessive salt to your child?

**Cereals.** Stay away from the extra sugary kinds. If you put some fruit on the various unsugared cereals, they taste fine and are far healthier.

I can almost hear you thinking, "But how can I deprive my little child of all these delicious treats?" An occasional "treat" is okay, but not as part of an everyday diet. Yes, you may be "depriving" your child by following my suggestions, but what you actually will be "depriving" him of is dental decay, obesity, early onset of heart disease, and high blood pressure. These are all important "deprivations."

If you look at your child and find he is too fat, do not automatically assume that the obesity will go away. The longer you allow him to remain fat, the more likely it is that he will be fat all his life. If this is the case in your house, check with his doctor and ask his advice. You will probably have to modify your child's diet and cut down on some calories, as well as increase his physical activity. This is easier to do now than later on, when he is more set in his eating and exercise patterns.

I would suggest that you do not waste your time trying to teach your child good table manners at this age. It just won't work. What you can do is set a proper example in terms of how you eat, and that is all. If you eat slowly, always sitting down while you eat, and chew your food slowly, chances are that your child will eventually learn to eat the same way. The entire family should eat together whenever possible, and every member should be served the same "prudent" type of diet described above.

More and more evidence continues to accumulate demonstrating how important proper nutrition is in terms of overall health and longevity. I believe that it is never too early to start your child on the road to correct eating.

### EXERCISE

Little children at this age love to run, jump, climb, and balance themselves. They can be taught to ride a tricycle and greatly enjoy all sorts of rhythmic play and dancing. They try very hard to exercise their large muscles by involving themselves in all sorts of vigorous activities. If you give your child the opportunity, he will happily spend many hours each day in an excellent continuing program of physical fitness. However, our culture makes it difficult for youngsters to exercise to the degree required to develop and maintain optimal physical fitness. The many work-saving conveniences which eliminate physical effort — the automobile, elevator, and escalator — all lead to a sedentary life-style. If you add to these factors the usual lack of encouragement to exercise in early life, the result is that many of our preschool children are not given sufficient opportunity to challenge their musculo-skeletal systems and so cannot achieve real physical vigor and well-being. Television plays an important part in interfering with good physical development. A child at this age who becomes accustomed to sitting in front of the television set for hours on end (often with a sugar-laden snack to keep him company) will undoubtedly continue to behave this way as he grows older. The results are obvious. By the time these inactive children are ready for school, they are already flabby, overweight, poorly coordinated, and unable to keep up with their more physically fit classmates.

If you don't want this to happen to your child, the time to do something about it is now. Encourage your child to exercise every chance he gets. Let him walk rather than ride in a car, walk up the stairs with you rather than take the elevator or escalator. Keep his television watching down to a reasonable amount of time, and, of course, be selective in what he watches (more about this in the mental development section). According to an interesting statistic that I came across recently, the average American child growing up spends more time watching television (15,000 hours) than in the classroom (11,000 hours).

Parents who truly have their children's best interests at heart must set proper examples. The sedentary, inactive life-style of the majority of adults in our society teaches their children that it is also perfectly acceptable for them to sit around much of the time. A recent survey conducted by the President's Council on Physical Fitness reflects this sorry state of affairs. This study showed that 45 percent of all adult Americans do not engage in any physical activity for the purpose of exercise. Even more significant is the fact that most of these nonexercisers believe that they are getting enough exercise. If you fall into this 45 percent group of nonexercisers, my advice is to change your ways, not only for your own health and well-being but also for your child's.

The Committee on Pediatric Aspects of Physical Fitness, Recreation and Sports of the Academy of Pediatrics recently pointed out a major flaw in our present system of health care. The emphasis in evaluating the health of a child is primarily on the presence or absence of disease, with little regard given to the quality of how he functions. An infant or child is considered healthy if he is fully immunized and free of any specific illness. This definition of optimal health is not complete. As part of the overall evaluation of the health status of the child, we should also ask and determine if he is able to meet his daily tasks, activities, and sudden emergencies with enthusiasm and vigor and without tiring too quickly. I believe that a child so "out of shape" that he can't keep up with his friends is just as unhealthy as if he is suffering from a particular illness.

Before going on to recommend specific exercises and activities for your two- to three-year-old, I want to call your attention to another important reason for encouraging your child to exercise (and to exercise more yourself). Many investigations have clearly demonstrated that exercise lowers both the blood cholesterol level and blood pressure. Further, exercise strengthens the heart muscles by increasing the collateral circulation to the heart. All this means that exercise protects against heart attacks. I once gave this lecture to an obese mother and father of a fat two-and-a-half-year-old. When I finished, Mr. A. responded with, "I can understand what you are saying about my wife and myself but, Dr. Eden, you certainly can't mean that Eric will get a heart attack if he doesn't exercise." Obviously, two- to three-year-olds don't have heart attacks, but if Eric does not start exercising soon, it is unlikely that he will ever get into proper physical condition, so he will in fact be facing a greater risk of developing a heart condition later in life.

The following are the physical activities, exercises, and equipment that I believe will help your child achieve real physical fitness.

*Climbing equipment.* We have already discussed this in previous chapters. I merely want to add here that the two- to three-year-old is fascinated by this type of equipment as well as by swings and slides. Playing on all this is splendid exercise. It strengthens his muscles and helps build up his coordination and agility. I would strongly recommend that these activities always be supervised in order to prevent serious accidents.

*Toy wheelbarrows and construction trucks.* Carrying and dumping sand, dirt, and toys is what a two- to three-year-old enjoys more than anything else. This is another fine way for him to develop his large muscles. It also is a form of make-believe play in that he imagines he really is "working."

*Tricycle.* Now is the time for you to supply your child with a tricycle. Between two and three years of age most chidren can be taught to use the pedals. After he masters this new skill, you will find it difficult to keep your child off his tricycle. This is good exercise for developing leg muscles and coordination. Again, make certain that he rides his tricycle on the sidewalk and in safe places. If not specifically warned over and over again, a child will take off into traffic.

*Toy tools and a toy workbench.* We have already discussed this. It is an excellent way to let off steam, burn up calories, and exercise. It is also useful for developing good hand/eye coordination.

165

**Coloring books.** I have included coloring books here because coloring is an activity that improves hand/eye coordination.

**Pulling wagons, large balls, and large blocks.** All these help your child's large-muscle development.

**Sports.** This is a good age to encourage the development of skills in various sports activities, especially those that your child can continue all his life. It is a bit too early to think about skiing, skating, bowling, tennis, or golf, but how about swimming, running, and hiking? Two- to three-year-olds can be taught to swim since they have no fear of the water. It is important that they not be rushed and that the instruction be supervised by an expert. Many YMCAs and other organizations have programs designed especially to teach little children how to swim. Some parents worry about chlorine in the pools. In my experience, this is seldom a problem.

Soccer is becoming very popular in the United States, and since a two- to three-year-old can kick a ball and run all day, this is an ideal sport for him. Your child probably can throw a ball and learn to catch one now. Engaging in throwing and catching with your child helps promote his physical fitness and coordination. It improves hand/eye coordination and, of course, his actual skill in learning to throw and catch. When he reaches "Little League" age, he will have a better chance of excelling. Don't neglect wrestling, which still is great fun and an excellent overall conditioner. Wrestling builds up strength, agility, and balance.

SAFETY TIPS

A two- to three-year-old child is extremely active and his actions are often unpredictable. Although he understands quite a bit, he still does not have the judgment or the experience to realize what is dangerous. In order to prevent accidents and injuries, your child needs your supervision and protection and some rules of behavior he can follow.

**In the automobile.** Over fifteen hundred children under four years of age die each year from automobile accidents. Most of these deaths are preventable. The great majority of preschool-age children ride in cars without using any type of safety restraints. Studies have proven that both the death and injury rates can be reduced by over 80 percent if a child's seat restraint is used. It is essential that you make certain that your child wears an approved automobile child restraint *every* time he rides in a car. You also should wear a seat belt or harness for your own safety as well as to set the proper example. Finally, don't speed; you will not only cut down on your gasoline consumption, but more important, you will protect the valuable cargo you are carrying.

**Animal bites.** Keep your child away from strange dogs and teach him never to tease an animal. Your child should learn not to play with a dog while the dog is eating and not to wake a sleeping dog suddenly.

**Play injuries.** Always check all your child's toys and playground equipment for sharp edges and small, easily swallowed parts. Tricycles and riding toys should only be used on sidewalks.

**Fires and burns.** This is the third-ranking cause of accidental death in children between one and thirteen years of age. Therefore make it a habit always to keep matches and cigarette lighters away from children. Purchase flame-retardant sleepwear for your child and don't allow your young child to turn on hot-water faucets.

**Drowning.** I have said this earlier but let me repeat it: *Never* leave your child alone in a bathtub, or in any other water, for that matter. If your child is on a boat with you, he should always wear his own flotation device. A statistic to keep in mind is that an average of twenty-five hundred children die each year in the United States as a result of drowning.

**Falls and cuts.** Store your scissors and knives out of sight and out of reach of your child. When possible, use safety-glass doors. Install guards on all windows, especially those above the first floor.

**Dangerous objects.** Always lock up dangerous tools and garden equipment. Keep your little child away from lawn mowers and power tools. I have seen many serious accidents involving both lawn mowers and power tools.

**Poisons.** I covered this subject in detail in the previous chapter. You must continue to be on the alert now, however, since the incidence of poisoning remains high in the two- to three-year-old group.

Most accidents are preventable. They usually result from inadequate supervision, carelessness, or an improperly child-proofed home. If you keep these safety tips in mind, your child will be much less likely ever to suffer a serious or catastrophic accident or injury.

## EMOTIONAL (SOCIAL) DEVELOPMENT

There are four important general areas related to the emotional development of the two- to three-year-old that I want to discuss before going on to list specific recommendations. These topics, all crucial in terms of your child's future personality, are toilet training, anger, body image, and the birth of another child.

## TOILET TRAINING

I believe that most children are ready to be trained at around two years of age, give or take a few months. It has been my experience that a great many parents are overly concerned and worried about what is in reality a simple and normal developmental process. It must be remembered that properly achieved toilet training is a great source of satisfaction for your child. Some children train themselves. Others require and deserve your help and guidance. The most important factor in toilet training is your attitude. Forty or fifty years ago many children were completely toilet trained by one year of age, and in many cases this was the result of rigid and at times coercive methods. We have since learned that these techniques sometimes resulted in psychological problems for the child later on. Therefore, in recent years the pendulum has swung in the opposite direction. Many parents now take what I consider an overly permissive attitude to toilet training and say, "Leave him alone; he will train himself when he is ready." Those in this laissez-faire group are afraid that any active intervention on their part will cause their child to become angry and hostile.

My position regarding toilet training is middle-of-the-road. I believe that the answer lies somewhere between total permissiveness and the unyielding, rigid approach of yesteryear. The proper approach to toilet training (and, incidentally, toward almost everything else related to your child) should be one of friendliness, encouragement, and interest, along with consistency and perseverance. Taking such a posture will not frustrate your child, nor will it allow the situation to get completely out of hand. On the contrary, this supportive attitude will help encourage your child to please you and will ultimately play an important part in building up his self-esteem and the vital, trusting bond between you that is so very important.

By age two, most children have some regularity in their bowel movements and also are aware of when they are about to move their bowels. This is the right time to start the toilet-training process. All you need to do is learn to recognize the warning signs your baby gives before defecating; the rest is simple. Now is the time to get out his potty chair and sit him down when he gives you the proper signal. You can also use a baby seat on the regular toilet seat (this takes up less room than a potty chair) as long as there is a foot rest so that his feet don't dangle. An encouraging, optimistic approach works best. It may take weeks and sometimes months before he is successful for the first time. When that red-letter day finally arrives, make a big fuss about it. Tell him how proud and happy you are of his accomplishment and what a big boy he is. It takes a great deal of patience on your part, but try to remember that you are not working against any deadline. Never chastise or yell at or punish him, and above all else never shame him when he fails. There is no reason to compete with your neighbor in terms of who gets his or her child trained first. Some children take longer than others to train — and so what? It is counterproductive in terms of your child's achieving emotional stability and self-confidence if you make him feel guilty when he does not succeed. I have taken care of many children, including my own two, who were not yet trained as they sat down proudly to cut their third birthday cakes, still wearing diapers under their party clothes. Take my word for it; they all become toilet trained sooner or later.

**Myth:** *Late toilet training is associated with low intelligence.* This is utter and complete nonsense. As I wrote in *Handbook for New Parents,* " . . . there is absolutely no relationship between late toilet training and lack of intelligence. [Your child] can still grow up to be a professor at M.I.T."

I have not discussed bladder training, since successful bowel training usually results in the simultaneous control of urination. Therefore, most of the time it is not necessary to do much about urine training. Two suggestions that you may find helpful in achieving urine control are, first, wait for your child to be dry for about two hours and then take him to the potty chair. Also, use training pants. A two-year-old child usually does not like a cold, wet diaper, and transferring to training pants at the age of two can act as a stimulus to more speedy training. Boys are usually slower than girls in establishing control of their urine. Just as with bowel-movement training, there will be many accidents with urination. Sooner or later your child will be successful. Nighttime bladder control comes last, and you should do nothing about it. Once again, time and patience will take care of this.

The process of toilet training should be thought of as a natural event in your child's life and of considerable importance to his normal emotional development. Properly helping him to succeed when he is able will help you to establish a strong, positive bond with your child. It will do a world of good in building up his self-esteem and self-image. An interested, friendly, consistent, and encouraging attitude is the key. You do not have to read entire books devoted to how to toilet train your child. All you need is common sense and the right approach.

171

ANGER

Handling your child's anger and aggression and disobedience at this age can be both difficult and distressing. Many of us were never taught how to handle anger during our own childhood. We have been made to believe that anger is bad and so we automatically feel guilty when we are angry, even if the anger is justified. If we could get rid of this notion once and for all, it would make it easier for us to deal with our children's angry outbursts and aggressive behavior. The goal really should not be to repress these angry feelings in our children but rather to accept these feelings as a fact of life and to help channel them toward constructive and positive goals instead.

In order for you to be able to respond sensibly to anger and aggression in your child, you must first understand some of the feelings within the child that trigger this behavior. His anger may be associated with failure or frustration, a feeling of lowered self-esteem, feelings of loneliness and neglect, or it may be related to anxiety. Anger may be associated with sadness, jealousy, depression, or feelings of overdependency and frustration. It is important to remember that little children have the very same feelings that we do. The difference is that the little child is not yet mature enough to handle many of these feelings except by expressing anger, aggression, and negative behavior. I might add that there are lots of adults who have never matured beyond this childish response.

As I already suggested in a discussion on discipline in a previous chapter, it is much better to try to teach your child right from wrong rather than automatically to punish him for his negative behavior. Always punishing a child when he is aggressive or angry is the wrong way to communicate to him what you really expect. Your child must be taught more acceptable methods of coping with and handling his anger. As I mentioned earlier, discipline means teaching rather than punishing.

Good discipline involves creating an atmosphere of firmness, fairness, and reason. Bad discipline represents harsh and inappropriate punishment. You should approach and accept your angry or disobedient child as a trusting human being with a problem. He has feelings that he must express one way or another.

The following are suggestions, some of which I have already written about, for dealing with the angry and disobedient child.

***Promises and rewards.*** These are much more effective than punishment. Always remember to keep your promises, and as a rule, don't use food as one of the rewards.

**Scene removal.** This method of discipline should not be viewed strictly as punishment, but rather as your way of saying to your child that his behavior at the time is unacceptable and therefore he must leave the scene. I would suggest that you save this method for important occasions such as, for example, when he is about to hurt himself or somebody else. To be at all effective, you should calmly separate him from the scene of his crime, without losing your own temper. If you are consistent, he will soon get the message.

**Explanations.** The two- to three-year-old child understands much of what you say to him. Help him understand the cause of his angry or aggressive behavior. It is amazing how quickly a child will react properly if he understands what actually frustrated him, especially if you do your explaining quickly and sympathetically.

**Listening.** Encourage your child to talk about his bad feelings. For example, if he hurts his hand, ask him to tell you about it. The verbal group of two- to three-year-olds find this approach useful. This method probably is more effective after the child is three years old and a better talker.

**Be sympathetic.** It is very useful for you to get into the habit of telling your child when he is acting up and that you understand his feelings of anger and frustration. Tell him that instead of screaming and yelling and hitting, you would like him to tell you in words what is bothering him. As he gets closer to age three, he will be better able to respond appropriately to this approach.

**Don't be afraid to say "no."** It is important that you set limits, clearly explain them to your child, and then stick to your word. He must understand that you will not tolerate unacceptable or antisocial behavior. If your two- to three-year-old insists on riding his tricycle out into the street despite your repeated warnings, it is time to stop reasoning with him. Giving him a firm smack across his backside and then taking the tricycle away for a few days will be much more effective.

### BODY IMAGE

Another aspect of building up self-esteem involves helping your child develop a positive body image by learning to admire and love his own body. Without a healthy body image it will be much more difficult for him to establish real feelings of self-worth and self-esteem. I believe that one of the important goals of all parents should be to make every possible effort to help their children feel comfortable and happy about their bodies. Now is not too early to begin. If you are successful in this undertaking, your child will become less vulnerable to other people's estimates of him and therefore less susceptible to possible future embarrassment and shame.

Many children grow up with negative feelings about their bodies, and too often their parents are unaware of the adverse psychological consequences that will follow. These children grow up with disturbed and sometimes even distorted images of themselves and inevitably suffer from a lowering of their self-esteem and self-confidence.

There are a number of reasons why so many children end up with negative feelings about their bodies and there are specific steps you can take to see to it that this does not happen. The first reason is related to our puritanical heritage, with its emphasis on the body as being inherently "dirty" and a source of evil and temptation. The mother who slaps her child's hand when he plays with his penis inadvertently helps to promote negative feelings in the child's mind about that particular "bad" part of his anatomy. Although you may find it difficult to do so (especially in front of company), let your child explore his body without interfering. Teach your child the words for all parts of his body, including his penis and testicles. If you have a girl, teach her the word vagina and not some nonsensical baby word for it. It is amazing how many different foolish synonyms are given for vagina and penis. I have been struck by how very few parents teach their two- to three-year-olds to use the proper words, but they have no trouble at all with eyes, ears, nose, and mouth. These mothers and fathers cannot accept the fact that those potentially sexual areas of the body are not evil or something to be ashamed of. If, as you read this, you realize that you belong to this "uptight" group, I would strongly suggest that you try not to instill these same attitudes in your child. Passing on to your child your perception of him as having a beautiful body, including all his parts, will give him the permission and encouragement to appreciate and become more comfortable with himself as he actually is. I understand that this is a tall order for some parents, but it is something to think about very seriously.

**Myth:** *Masturbation in a little child is unhealthy, a sign of emotional trouble, or a sign of being oversexed.* All wrong. Masturbation during the first few years of life is a harmless habit and does not hurt the child in any way. It should be considered normal behavior and does not warrant scolding, punishment, or instilling guilt. The masturbating will stop sooner or later, and there is no reason to worry about it.

The other main reasons leading to the formation of a negative body image have already been covered in the physical development section of this chapter. One is our sedentary life-style, with its lack of exercise. This leads to flabbiness, clumsiness, obesity, and poor muscle tone. Another is related to the foods we eat, a diet too high in calories, fats, and refined sugars. Although a two- to three-year-old who is too fat will not worry about it yet, if he stays fat long enough, he will eventually face it in the form of ridicule, shame, and embarrassment as a schoolboy or adolescent. It makes little difference which comes first, the obesity or the negative body image; one goes right along with the other.

Not enough emphasis has been placed on the importance of helping children develop a good feeling about their bodies. There is little question that distorted and disturbed body images lead to emotional difficulties. It is important that you take the necessary steps *now* to promote a positive body image and a positive self-concept in your little child. If you succeed, you will have taken a big step in insuring that he will end up with increased emotional stability and soundness and with an increased zest for life.

## THE BIRTH OF ANOTHER CHILD

You may have noticed that up until now we have approached the subject of raising your child as if he were an only child. If you have been reading this book as a parent of more than one child, you have already realized how much more difficult it is to give time and attention to your baby with an older sibling or two or three around. If this is the case, you also have had experience dealing with jealousies and conflicts between them. But if you have a two- to three-year-old and are thinking about having another child, or if you are pregnant or have just given birth to a new baby, what I have to say now may be more meaningful.

"Dr. Eden, my Johnny is two and a half years old. Do you think it's a good idea for me to have another baby because we want Johnny to have company?" My answer to that mother was that although it is true a new baby certainly will be good company for Johnny, that is not in itself a good enough reason for deciding to have another baby. If that is your only reason for wanting another child, I would advise you to reconsider your decision.

"What is the ideal spacing between children?" As far as I am concerned, there is no such thing. While it is true that the rivalry between children who are less than three years apart is often more intense than that between children spaced farther apart, I don't believe that this factor should enter very seriously into your decision. Whatever the age differences between your children, there will always be some jealousy and rivalry. My brother is five and a half years older than I, and as I recall, we fought with each other throughout my childhood. My own two children are two and a half years apart and they fought with each other throughout their childhoods. Sibling rivalry must be accepted as normal, healthy behavior. It simply represents competition between children. Fighting between siblings can never be eliminated, but it can be minimized if you understand what is going on.

Assuming that your two- to three-year-old, without having asked for one, is presented with a baby brother or sister, how will he feel and act and how should you deal with these feelings and actions?

First of all, he will feel abandoned when his mother leaves him to go to the hospital to have the new baby. It will help if this doesn't come as a complete surprise to him. It is wiser to give him some prior warning about what is going to happen. This reminds me of the mother of a two-and-a-half-year-old boy who visited her obstetrician and was told that she was six weeks pregnant. She could not wait to get home and spring the good news on her son. This is ridiculous; your child does not need that much notice. It is a better idea to wait until one to two months before your delivery date and then tell him about it. Of course, if he notices your changing body shape and asks you why you are becoming so fat, it's time to explain about the new baby. When you do go to the hospital, talk to him about it, and if possible, arrange for him to visit you there. Unfortunately, most hospital maternity units do not allow two- to three-year-old visitors. If this is the case, a good compromise would be to phone him each day from your hospital bed. This will lessen his anxiety and feelings of desertion.

Your child's second reaction will be jealousy of all the attention heaped on the new and, from his point of view, unwanted member of the family. I would suggest that you come home from the hospital with two presents: one, the new baby, and the other, a special toy for your older child. It is also good practice to keep on hand a number of other presents, to be given to him each time a visitor brings a gift for the new baby.

Third, your child will be upset because you are now spending some of your time with the new baby. This cannot be helped, and there is no reason for you to feel guilty about it. Try your best to allocate a separate time away from the new baby for your two- to three-year-old. Since you have already had previous experience with a new baby, you will probably be more efficient now and so will be able to find the time. Whenever possible, take him out of the house alone without the new baby for an automobile ride, to the supermarket, to the park, etc. Use these times to remind him that he is the *big* brother.

Another reaction of your two- to three-year-old will be anger and hostility. Accept this as a normal reaction to a situation he does not like. Limits must be set. No matter how angry or jealous he may be, hitting the new baby is completely unacceptable. Tell your child that it is okay to become angry, but hitting and hurting are out. An attuned and sympathetic mother once taught me a constructive way to help handle the problem of jealousy. She told me that she made it her business to criticize her new baby from time to time while the older child was around. She would chastise and scold the new baby for such things as having a dirty diaper, crying, refusing his food, and the like, and her

**177**

older child would carefully observe all this and would feel much better. I will never forget what she said: "If he knew the words, he would say, 'Well, well, there really is some justice in the world.'"

When another baby is born, your child may regress in his behavior. During my telephone advice hour one morning I heard the following from a flabbergasted mother: "Our new baby has been home exactly three days and Dennis [age two years, nine months] is already back into diapers and stealing the new baby's bottle." I advised this mother and I am advising you not to be concerned about this regressive behavior. If you keep yourself from criticizing your child with such statements as "I am ashamed of you," or "You are a big boy," or "Don't act like a big baby," and simply leave him alone, he will rapidly revert back to his normal, more mature ways.

Finally, I would advise you to attempt to involve your two- to three-year-old in helping with the new baby. He really can be very useful in many ways. Tell him how much you and the new baby appreciate his assistance. Showing him how much you appreciate his help and how important he is to you will help minimize his feelings of hostility and jealousy toward the new star attraction.

## SPECIFIC SUGGESTIONS

The following are my recommendations for specific activities to help your two- to three-year-old better achieve emotional stability and maturity now and in the future.

**Fears.** All children develop fears of one kind or another and there is no way you can prevent them. However, you can help your child overcome these fears — of the dark, of separation, of nightmares, of death, and of sudden loud noises — if you first accept his fears as being something very real to him. They should never be ignored or laughed off. Whenever possible, take your child away from the frightening situation and then, after he has calmed down, talk to him about it and listen to him as he tries to express his feelings to you. By being calm and sympathetic and by helping him face his fears, you will do much to help him overcome them more quickly. If he is successful in handling the fear, his self-confidence will be built up along with his feelings of trust in you. He will look upon you as somebody he can turn to for support in times of stress and trouble.

**"Dress-up" clothes.** This is an excellent activity for make-believe play, and children love it. Take your choice, but mine is hats — all sorts of hats. The more, the merrier! One of the funniest home movies I have ever taken was of our daughter, age two and a half, in our back yard trying on one different hat after another as fast as she could, hamming it up and laughing with glee at each and every change.

**Toy trains.** Your two- to three-year-old should be ready for toy trains that he can hook together and take apart himself. After you show him how they work, all he needs is a conductor's hat and he is ready to take off (in his mind) on all sorts of wonderful trips. Yes, Dad, it's too early for you to buy him electric trains!

**Wooden and plastic blocks.** These remain ideal for imaginative and creative play. Your child can build forts and towers and buildings; then he can knock them down and begin all over again.

**Finger puppets.** Many children in this age group have a great deal of fun with puppets. They can be taught to manipulate them, and it is a fine way for children to exercise their imaginations and their creativity.

**Painting.** Your child can be given a paint brush or he can use his fingers or he can use both. I have to admit that finger painting, although a fine outlet for your child to express his feelings, can get pretty messy. If he does finger paint, be sure to spread plenty of newspapers on the floor — and I would advise you not to dress him up in his Sunday finest. In *Teach Your Baby to Talk,* Dr. Pushaw suggests using chocolate pudding on wax paper for finger painting. It sounds like a fine idea. If the child isn't happy with what he has painted, he can eat it up and start all over.

**Pasting.** This is another messy but useful activity for your child's emotional development. Pasting is similar to painting in that it is an expressive experience for him. It is another way for him to let out his feelings. One easy method to make paste is by mixing flour, salt, and water.

**Singing.** At this age children love to imitate, and they are ready and more than willing to sing along with you. Some favorite songs that you can sing together are, "Row, row, row your boat," "Twinkle, twinkle little star," and "Jingle bells."

**Dancing.** I consider this an important and often neglected activity. Dancing will do wonders for a child's body image, self-expression, and feelings. Also, it is a fine form of exercise. You can make up dances together, dancing in time to the music. Your child can dance to show

how he feels. Parents who are not comfortable dancing themselves find this a difficult activity. If you and your child are alone, there is no possible reason to feel embarrassed. Just relax and let yourself go in time to the music and your child will do the same. I believe that dancing allows a child to become more comfortable with his own body and this good feeling (positive body image) will stay with him as he grows and matures.

**Rhythmic instruments.** I am referring to pots, pans, and spoons; with these instruments a child has the opportunity to bang away and march around the room to his heart's content. It might be wise to get yourself a set of ear plugs if you are not into this type of music.

**Coloring books.** This is another aspect of creative and imaginative play. After he has had the opportunity to do his coloring, it is a good idea to talk with your child about what he has done. If you take one of his masterpieces and tack it up on the wall of his room, it will make him very happy and proud. While it hangs there it will serve as a constant reminder of his fine accomplishment. This is splendid for building up his self-esteem.

**Scrapbook.** At this age your child can start putting together his own scrapbooks by finding pictures in magazines and pasting them into his own book. This can be an interesting project and it should be all his own, although you will be needed to cut out the pictures. Such an activity is useful in terms of developing feelings of independence.

**Clay and Play-doh.** These materials have already been taken up in the previous chapter. They remain excellent vehicles for your child to express his feelings through imaginative play. As he develops more strength and dexterity in his fingers, he will become more and more successful in creating all sorts of interesting shapes and objects.

**Water play.** Your child will continue to enjoy playing with and in water. You can supply him with some floating toys and let him splash around to his heart's content. Another interesting water-play activity requires a plastic straw and some soap flakes. You can then show him how to blow bubbles. This is a really sloppy activity, so I would suggest that after he is finished, you give him the chore of cleaning up the mess he is sure to have made.

**Blackboard.** Many parents do not think of this one. I would strongly advise you to buy a large blackboard which will give your child plenty of space to do his work. The best place to hang it is on a wall in his room. Supply him with pieces of different-colored chalk and he is in business. A blackboard is ideal for imaginative and creative drawing, and it also allows him to develop the skill of holding the chalk and manipulating it properly. This will make it easier for him to learn to handle the pencils and pens which will be such an important part of his armamentarium in school. I would suggest that you carefully explain to him that the chalk is to be used only on the blackboard. Mrs. W. told me about her little fellow, who had a lapse of memory about this instruction. What John did was to use his chalk to create a full-length mural covering the entire wall of his parents' newly-painted bedroom.

**Sharing.** As I have already explained, two- to three-year-olds are basically egocentric or self-centered. They really are not very generous when it comes to sharing their possessions. While in the company of other children they play alongside rather than with them. Nevertheless, I believe that at this age sharing is an important concept for them to start to learn. The best time to teach your child about sharing is while there are other little children around. Get him accustomed to the idea of sharing his toys with his friends. There will be much less trouble if you have enough toys to go around. Explain to him that sharing is the right thing to do, and if he goes along with you, tell him how very happy his behavior has made you.

**Silence.** In *How to Parent,* Dr. Dodson describes an activity he calls the "silence game." This is good training for your child in terms of his schooling later on since it is designed to teach him to remain quiet and listen without talking—which is universally appreciated by teachers everywhere. To start with, tell him that you are about to play a game with him. This is very important because if he thinks it's a game he will pay attention to the instructions. Explain that the game is for both of you to sit quietly without saying a word and just listen for sounds. Then you say, "Now tell me what you hear." Try whispering an instruction to him or ask him to shut his eyes and tell you what noise you are making. Then you whistle or clap your hands or snap your fingers. I have suggested this game to many parents and they tell me that it usually is a big success. Probably the best time to play it is shortly before reading your child his bedtime story, since it will serve to quiet him down gradually from his hard day of vigorous, noisy, stimulating activity.

**TV.** I am including television in the section on emotional development to remind you how susceptible and vulnerable your little child is to what he sees and hears on TV. I am referring particularly to the association of television and violence. Many studies have shown that viewing violence on TV produces increased aggressive behavior in the young child. The estimate is that the average child will see eighteen thousand murders on television by the time he finishes high school. As your child grows older it will become more difficult for you to monitor his television watching. At this age, it should not be much of a problem. You must decide and control what programs your child will watch. While he is watching, you should observe how he is reacting to what he is seeing on the television screen. If you notice that he gets too excited or confused or upset, it is the wrong program for him and should be turned off. This is unlikely to happen if you have been selective and allow him to watch only some of the excellent children's television programs such as "Sesame Street" and "Captain Kangaroo."

## MENTAL (INTELLECTUAL) DEVELOPMENT

In the previous chapter I discussed the dangers of overburdening your child's mental capacities. I want to remind you again that too much of a good thing is just as bad as too little. Because of the competitive pressures of our society, many parents simply try too hard to raise a brighter child, a child who will be better able to handle the rigorous intellectual demands of our educational system. Since academic achievement is seen as a major indicator of success in our culture, many parents fall into the trap of trying too hard by attempting to teach their children more than they can handle.

Years ago the consensus was that good old common sense was all that was required to raise a child properly. We now believe that it takes more than that to give your child the best possible start. The entire thrust of this book has been to give you the added information and insight that are needed along with your own common sense to help make you the best possible parent. As I have done in each of the previous chapters, I will be offering you specific recommendations to help your child develop his optimum intellectual potential. But before doing so I want to caution you not to expect or demand too much too soon. How can a parent realize when he or she is pushing a child too hard? Probably the best way is just by watching and listening to him. If he is happy with what you are doing together, you can rest assured that he is not being taxed beyond his mental capabilities. Stimulate and challenge his mind, but give him tasks at which he can succeed. Provide him with problem-solving situations that he can handle, and praise him each time he is successful. I believe that this is the ideal learning environment for a child and the best way to insure his subsequent success in school.

Dr. Gesell, the famous child psychologist, uses the expression "word hungry" to describe the language development of the two- to three-year-old. This child is now anxious to learn more and more words, so any type of word game that you can think of will help satisfy his hunger for new words and new phrases. One of the keys to effective language acquisition is to play word games in which the child is asked questions about the world around him. It is clear that children learn language best in the context of their family life and you, the parents, act as the models they imitate. If you have a tendency to use baby talk, the result will be that your child will continue to use immature speech. It is important to use correct English when you talk to him. Ask and answer his questions without using baby talk. By doing so, you will more rapidly improve his primitive language. For example, if he says, "Where doggy is?" you can say, "Where is your dog? He is in the kitchen."

"Dr. Eden, Michael is driving me crazy," said a harassed mother to me. "He keeps asking me questions from morning until night. I feel guilty when I just don't have the time or strength to answer him." I assured her that it is both impossible and unnecessary to answer all his questions. There is no sense feeling guilty about this. All that can be expected of you is to do the best you can within the limits of your time and patience. When you do answer a question, make it short and simple. Your child is not interested in a long, elaborate, detailed answer. Also, don't be upset with him if he asks the same question over and over again. You would do well to remember that his memory is far from perfect. What he needs is small amounts of simple, clear information repeated at different times.

Your two- to three-year-old realizes that now everything has a name, and he wants to learn them all. You will notice that he will spend a great deal of time practicing words, just as he previously spent a great deal of his time practicing climbing up and down the stairs. When he correctly answers a question or learns a new word or new phrase, make certain that he knows you approve of his accomplishment.

Besides asking him questions, another effective method of helping him learn language is to repeat thoughts frequently in different contexts. Let us use a toy car as an example. You can say, "Here is the car." Next time, say, "Let's make the car run." You can then put the car away and say, "I don't see the car." Then bring the car back and run it along the floor, imitating the noise of the motor, and say, "The car makes a noise when it runs."

Above all, do not try to rush or push your child's speech development. Each child learns at his own individual pace. Make sure that your efforts to help him learn language remain fun. You can certainly help him develop language competence, but don't be frantic about it. Although some verbally precocious two- to three-year-olds can actually be taught to read, as a general rule I would discourage you from trying during this year. It is simply too early and usually is a complete waste of time.

By age three, many children will have a vocabulary of up to one thousand words and also will be able to put together a number of short, complex sentences. Often the child's language will be both imaginative and logical. There are times when his language will be more descriptive than your own. Two recent examples of this come to mind. A three-year-old who saw his bald-headed uncle come into the room pointed immediately to the bald scalp and said, "Skin-head." And a two-and-a-half-year-old who was playing in the park when a really obese lady came into view ran over to her and said at the top of his lungs, "Mommy, look at the big, round lady." Listen to your child carefully when he speaks. He may come up with some priceless sayings.

Many parents are overly concerned when their children mispronounce various sounds. By their third birthdays the majority of children make the following sounds correctly: mmm, nnn, ng, f, p, and h. They usually cannot as yet pronounce sss, sh, ch, wh, b, k, g, or r.

There is no reason to worry if your child cannot articulate certain sounds at this age. By the time he starts school his speech pattern will be greatly improved. If you have any questions about how his speech is developing, consult your doctor.


SPECIFIC SUGGESTIONS

The following are specific suggestions and recommendations which I believe will help your child develop his intellectual capabilities to the fullest.

**Jigsaw puzzles.** Simple jigsaw puzzles without too many different pieces are readily available. These are usually made out of wood or sturdy plastic. Jigsaw puzzles are challenging to your child and enjoyable for him to solve. Besides complimenting him when he succeeds in putting one together, you should talk with him about the object that the completed puzzle represents.

**Clay and Play-doh.** I have included these in this section because they can help your child in his language development. Words such as top, side, flat, round, smooth, and rough should be used when you talk to him about what he has created.

**Crayons and pencils.** Supply your child with large sheets of paper and a good-sized crayon or pencil. Most two- to three-year-olds spend happy time scribbling away, and this is good practice for their future writing and drawing. These little children are very proud of what they have "written" on the paper, so when your child brings his handiwork to you for approval, tell him what a good job he has done. There will be times when, with some imagination on your part, you may be able to pick out a specific object that he unintentionally drew on the scribbled page. If this occurs, show it to him and talk to him about it. He may try to do it again but it's unlikely that he will succeed.

**Instructions.** At this age your child's mind is sophisticated enough to follow more than one instruction at a time. He can understand and remember rather complicated directions. Instead of simply asking him to do one particular chore and then, after he has completed it, to do another, give him a larger challenge. For example, the following is not beyond the mental capability of most two- and three-year-olds: "Go to your room and bring back your toy teddy and then put it on the sofa." Your child may get it right the first time. If he mixes up the directions, repeat the same set of instructions, but always without showing anger or disappointment. When he does it right, celebrate his accomplishment with a big hug and tell him how well he has done.

**Bedtime ritual.** This is excellent not only in terms of your child's emotional security, but also for learning. Children look forward to the bedtime routine and it is an ideal way to end each of their days. To help your little child wind down and prepare for sleep, eliminate roughhouse activities and television-watching before bedtime. More appropriate activities are taking a bath, then eating a snack, and finally reading a story while he is in bed. *A Parent's Guide to Children's Reading,* by Dr. Nancy Larrick, is an excellent source for children's books of all ages. Read him a story appropriate for his age that he is interested in. Show him the pictures and ask him questions about what you have been reading. As an alternative, you can make up your own story. I remember a running serial that I continued for months on end when our son was this age. He would remind me where I stopped the night before if I forgot or started off in the wrong place.

**Trips.** Take advantage of your child's inexhaustible zest for new experiences by taking him out on as many trips as you possibly can. These trips will expand his horizons and stimulate his brain, and are extremely important in helping him learn as much as possible while having a good time. I am referring to trips such as to the zoo, library, and museum. Take him to the firehouse and to construction sites so that he can watch and learn about people working. There is also nothing wrong with taking him to a restaurant. It is amazing how well-behaved most two- or three-year-olds are in a restaurant. I would hesitate to pick an elegant, expensive French restaurant as his first experience, but there is certainly no reason to automatically assume that your child will only enjoy one of the fast-food places. Try also not to select a time when service may be slow, as children of this age find long periods of sitting and waiting difficult.

**Children's records.** Many excellent children's records are available and these are certainly a good vehicle for learning.

**Children's books with pictures.** I have already referred to these as they relate to the bedtime ritual. Obviously, children should be read to at other times too. The more books in the house, the better. One of the major cornerstones of your child's learning is your reading and explaining and asking questions about what you have read. These reading sessions always stop at the first sign of his boredom or disinterest.

**Television.** Up until now, all I have written about television has been negative. However, in terms of your child's intellectual development there is little question that television can play a useful role if used sensibly. The problem for you is to spend the time to find the few good children's programs and not allow your child to waste many hours watching cartoons or television programs filled with violence. Selected children's television programs have been shown to be an important educational tool. When at all possible, I would suggest that you watch these programs along with your child and ask him to try some of the activities he sees on the programs. He will learn much more if you are there to answer his questions and stimulate his interest.

***Word games.*** I have referred to word games in the introduction to this chapter. Since your two- to three-year-old is so anxious to learn new words and new phrases, he will be more than ready for this type of activity. For example, point to a ball and say, "I see something round. What is it?" or say, "It's cold today. What should we wear when we go out?" The possibilities for these word-game activities are endless, and they do much to develop and enhance your child's language and thinking skills.

***Self-correction.*** In *Teach Your Child to Talk,* David Pushaw suggests that by making an occasional speech mistake yourself, you can indirectly

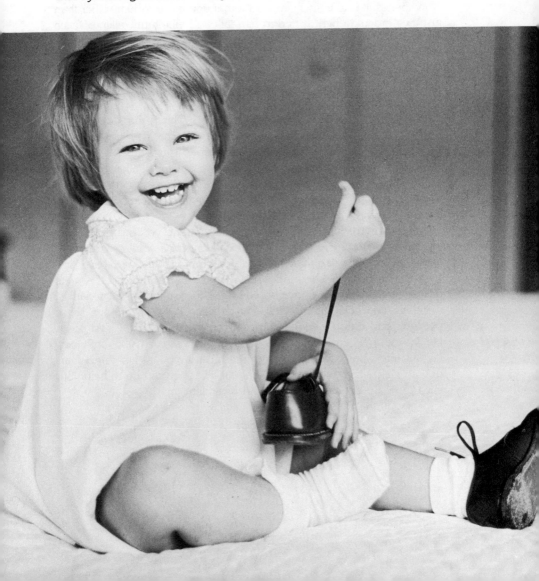

teach your child that it is acceptable for him to make mistakes without worrying too much about them. This is an interesting concept and makes a good deal of sense, provided you don't do it too often or make a game of it. For example, you can say, "Where is 'poon?" "No, not 'poon. Where is spoon?" If he sees that you are not infallible, it will be easier for him to practice his language and not be overly concerned about the mistakes he makes. Again, rather than criticizing him when he is wrong, correct him instead.

***Conversation and discussion.*** Between two and three years of age, two-way conversation between you and your child is still rather limited. Nonetheless, it is extremely important that you talk *with* him rather than just give orders to him. Listen to him talk and take turns talking. Teach him as you talk together. For example, if he says, "See doggy," you say, "Yes, I see the dog. He barks." He will often mix up the word order and you should correct him by then saying the words in their right order. It is not necessary to always ask him to repeat it correctly. He will learn for himself in time.

Mealtimes should be used for discussion. This is the ideal time to ask your child about what he has done and seen that day. Give him the chance to talk about his experiences as best he can. Rather than trying to keep him quiet so that he can concentrate on eating, allow him to be more of an active participant in these mealtime conversations. Talking together like this has been shown conclusively to be an important factor in school achievement.

**Final myth:** *In order to be a positive parent, you must be highly educated and you must supply your child with all sorts of elaborate, expensive equipment and toys.* Wrong on both counts. If you have read through this book, it should be obvious that you do not need a great deal of formal education, nor do you need to buy lots of fancy games, materials, and equipment. What you do need is some common sense plus guidance, information, and recommendations to do the best possible job as a parent. I hope that this book has given you both new insights into what goes on during these most important first three years of your child's life, and knowledge about what you can do to help your child grow up brighter, happier, and healthier.

Happy third birthday!

# Epilogue

# The Twelve Commandments
## of
## Positive Parenting

1. Challenge and stimulate the mind.
2. Overburdening must be avoided.
3. Make it easy for curiosity and independence to flourish.
4. Make certain that you set proper examples.
5. Admire and build up their self-esteem.
6. Never hit or abuse in anger.
7. Don't set unrealistic goals.
8. Make available the proper tools, activities, space, and opportunities.
9. Encourage exercise and physical fitness and a nutritious diet.
10. Nurture them with love and laughter.
11. Trust them.
12. Spend "quality time" together.

# Recommended Reading List

*The First Twelve Months of Life,* by Frank Caplan (Grosset & Dunlap)
*The Second Twelve Months of Life,* by Frank Caplan and Theresa Caplan (Grosset & Dunlap)
*The First Three Years of Life,* by Burton White (Prentice-Hall, Inc.; Avon Books)
*Help Your Baby Learn,* by Stephen Lehane (Prentice-Hall, Inc.)
*Teach Your Baby to Talk,* by David Pushaw (Dantree Press)
*Your Child's Self-Esteem,* by Dorothy Briggs (Doubleday & Co.; Dolphin Books)
*How to Parent,* by Fitzhugh Dodson (Nash Publishing; Signet Books)
*Supertot,* by Jean Marzollo (Harper Colophon Books)
*Baby Learning Through Baby Play,* by Ira V. Gordon (St. Martin's Press)
*Parenting,* by Sidney Callahan (Doubleday & Co.; Penguin Books)
*The Magic Years,* by Selma Fraiberg (Charles Scribner's Sons)
*How to Raise a Human Being,* by Lee Salk and Rita Kramer (Warner Books)
*Piaget's Theory of Intellectual Development,* by Herbert Ginsburg and Sylvia Opper (Prentice-Hall, Inc.)
*A Primer of Infant Development,* by T.E.R. Bower (W. N. Freeman & Co.)
*Readings in Child Development,* by Irving Weiner and David Elkind (John Wiley & Sons)
*Child Safety is No Accident,* by Jay Arena and Miriam Bachar (Duke University Press)
*A Piaget Primer,* by Dorothy Singer and Tracey Revenson (International Universities Press)

# Index